KV-373-658

CAPE VERDE

**Travel with Marco Polo
Insider Tips**

MARCO POLO
TOP HIGHLIGHTS

DELGADIM ⭐
Steep drops both to the left and right: take the road along a high ridge with sensational views.

➤ p. 96, Northern Islands

RIBEIRA DO PAÚL ⭐
Gigantic trees, rustling sugar cane and gurgling water in a lush tropical valley.
📷 *Tip: It's difficult to capture a panoramic image of the incredible mountain landscape, but more detailed shots will always work.*

➤ p. 98, Northern Islands

PICO DO FOGO ⭐
You will never forget the speedy descent through vast ash fields (photo)!
📷 *Tip: At sunrise, the shadow of the Pico is projected onto the opposite caldera wall.*

➤ p. 81, Southern Islands

PRAIA DA VARANDINHA ⭐
Drive off-road through barren dunes to this dreamy beach.

➤ p. 58, Eastern Islands

PRAIA DE SANTA MARIA ⭐
The white fairy-tale beach on Sal is popular with bathers and sun worshippers.

➤ p. 50, Eastern Islands

CIDADE VELHA ⭐
In the footsteps of Columbus and Vasco da Gama: this is where the colonisation of the tropics began.
📷 *Tip: The dilapidated ruin of the cathedral looks most atmospheric in the afternoon light.*

➤ p. 72, Southern Islands

SÃO FILIPE ⭐
Picturesque town with elegant colonial houses and a strong North American influence.

➤ p. 78, Southern Islands

DESERTO DE VIANA 🟊 8
If you see a camel, it's bound to be a mirage; otherwise, the desert feeling between white scythe-shaped dunes and a shimmering horizon is all real.

➤ p. 54, Eastern Islands

MINDELO 🟊 9
Working folk, yacht owners, artists and spivs: opposites attract and that's what the Cape Verdean (music) metropolis is all about.
📷 *Tip: Doors, balcony railings, windows – such details will add flair to your shots of the colonial architecture.*

➤ p. 104, Northern Islands

CARBERINHO 🟊 10
A phenomenal rocky landscape with thundering fountains of ocean spray and salt crunching underneath your feet.
📷 *Tip: Walk up close – the bizarre stone sculptures carved out of the steep cliffs by water and wind are a spectacular sight.*

➤ p. 116, Northern Islands

CONTENTS

CONTENTS

🕑   Plan your visit

€–€€€   Price categories

(*)   Premium-rate phone number

🍴   Eating/drinking

👜   Shopping

🍸   Nightlife

🏖️   Best beaches

    Rainy day activities

    Budget activities

    Family activities

🚩   Classic experiences

(📖 A2) Refers to the removable pull-out map
(📖 a2) Refers to the additional map on the pull-out map
(0) Located off the map

Palmeira, Sal Island

BEST OF
CAPE
VERDE

The bay of São Pedro on Ilha de São Vicente is not always this deserted

BEST
IN THE HEAT

BEAUTIFUL EVEN WHEN IT'S HOT

SLOWING DOWN
Before you enter *Viveiro Eco Park*, have a look around and see how barren the land is. Then, once inside, you will appreciate this small green oasis. The shady refuge on Sal, with its many plants and animals, is a place to both slow down and cool down.
➤ p. 45, Eastern Islands

DIVE IN
On a half-day sailing trip with *Cabo Kai Tours* on the *Spöki* off the coast of Boa Vista, you can feel the wind in your hair before diving into the ocean. You will be mesmerised by the spectacular underwater world.
➤ p. 56, Eastern Islands

FROM FISHING LINES TO DENTURES
Sucupira are local markets for clothes, shoes, electronic equipment, CDs, household utensils, car supplies and much more (photo). There is plenty to see – live animals, colourful shoes, bright African fabrics – and you can often find beautiful things. The largest covered *sucupira* is in Praia.
➤ p. 71, Southern Islands

TREES & FLOWERS
A stroll through the *Botanical Garden* in São Jorge dos Orgãos will serve as an introduction to Cape Verde's endemic plants, medicinal herbs and various tree species.
➤ p. 72, Southern Islands

PEACE, QUIET & CULTURE
The airy courtyard in the *Centro Cultural de Mindelo* is the perfect place to sit down and relax or to enjoy one of the changing exhibitions. A small shop sells a wide selection of Cape Verdean handicrafts.
➤ p. 106, Northern Islands

BEST 🐷
ON A BUDGET

FOR SMALLER WALLETS

ART

If you are interested in Cape Verdean culture, the *Palácio da Cultura Ildo Lobo* in Praia is the place to go for the contemporary art scene. There are free photo and art exhibitions, concerts, theatre productions, workshops and more.

➤ p. 70, Southern Islands

BIRTHDAY CELEBRATION

Live music galore – Cape Verde's capital city Praia celebrates the anniversary of its foundation on 19 May. To mark the occasion, dozens of bands, DJs and thousands of visitors come together to celebrate enthusiastically for the free, three-day *music festival*.

➤ p. 76, Southern Islands

AIDE-MEMOIRE

Monique Widmer has been collecting historical objects and documents dealing with everyday life on the islands of Cape Verde – especially on Fogo – for more than 25 years. Furniture, household effects, old photos and other interesting exhibits tell the turbulent history of the islands in her *Casa da Memória*, and there is no admission charge.

➤ p. 78, Southern Islands

FULL MOON FESTIVAL

Entrance to the *music festival in Baía das Gatas* is free! Every year, bands from Cape Verde, Africa and Latin America perform for three days – on the first weekend in August after the full moon – on São Vicente's most famous beach.

➤ p. 111, Northern Islands

A LITTLE NIGHT MUSIC

Live music as a free extra with your dinner – these are the *noites caboverdeanas* in Mindelo – where you can dine, chat and enjoy the soulful background music as an accompaniment (photo).

➤ p. 112, Northern Islands

BEST WITH CHILDREN

FUN FOR YOUNG & OLD

HORSE RIDING
A tour at walking pace on horseback for around five hours along the azure-blue Atlantic and back through a beautiful dune landscape is suitable for beginners and children. At *Santa Marilha Horse Excursions* on Sal.
➤ p. 48, Eastern Islands

INTO THE SEA!
You need patience to watch when giant turtles lay their eggs in the sand at night, and this is more of an activity for adults. However, being present when the turtle babies are released back into the ocean is fun for children as well; available at the *Project Biodiversity* on Sal.
➤ p. 49, Eastern Islands

NEW LOOK
Airy, practical and an entirely new look: having had their hair braided in multiple tiny plaits and adorned with colourful beads, your children will suddenly look very different after a *visit to the market* in Praia and may even be hard to recognise!
➤ p. 71, Southern Islands

DONKEY HIKING
The kids (max. 40kg) ride the donkeys, while you walk alongside with a guide on the *old mule paths* of Santo Antão. Splendid!
➤ p. 102, Northern Islands

FEASTING & BATHING
The four-star *Hotel Foya Branca* in São Pedro on São Vicente welcomes non-guests to a lavish Sunday lunch buffet including use of the outdoor facilities with three swimming pools – one of which is reserved for children.
➤ p. 108, Northern Islands

STRATEGIC MOVES

A typical scene: two men sitting in the shade with a wooden board between them, pondering over how they can get as many "seeds" as possible away from their opponent. The game is called *oril* (photo) and it attracts many players and spectators in locations such as the town centre of *Espargos* on Sal.

➤ p. 45, Eastern Islands

SWING THOSE HIPS

You won't know what has hit you when the dancers start swinging their hips at a dizzying speed dancing the *batuco* in the *5al da Música* in Praia.

➤ p. 76, Southern Islands

A HEARTY DELIGHT

The Cape Verde national dish *cachupa* is a hearty affair. Every cook prepares their own different version of this stew made of sweetcorn and beans – in *Fronteira* on Fogo they add pumpkin.

➤ p. 82, Southern Islands

PURE FIREWATER

No matter whether it is freshly distilled or aged, the Cape Verde sugar cane liquor packs a punch! The freshly brewed firewater *(grogue novo)* that is served in the traditional distillery of *Ildo Benrós* on Santo Antão and elsewhere will really take your breath away!

➤ p. 98, Northern Islands

TRAVEL WITH THE LOCALS

The *aluguer* is the most common means of transport in Cape Verde. You should travel at least once with the locals in one of these minibuses or pickups, but the journey only starts when all seats are taken.

➤ p. 130, Good to know

GET TO KNOW CAPE VERDE

A trader on her way to the market in Sal Rei

Beach joggers and water-sports fans love the "desert island" of Boa Vista

DISCOVER CAPE VERDE

People rarely rush on Cape Verde. Taking it easy is the name of the game. In Cape Verde you go with the flow of life, as long as you keep your head above water. If you come across an obstacle, find a way around it, but stay calm and relax!

TIME + QUIET = RELAXATION

Colourful fishing boats lie on the white sandy beaches, the deep-blue ocean glitters as far as the eye can see, while a gentle breeze cools off the scorching sun. The village square and the narrow, cobbled streets seem to be deserted; only a few children can be seen playing with their homemade toys. However, there is a lot of hustle and bustle at the vegetable market – the centre and heart of every village – loud shouting and laughter, friendly faces and mountains of fresh fruit.

From 1456
The Portuguese discover and colonise Cape Verde

1461
Ribeira Grande is the first settlement on Santiago

1466
Ribeira Grande is granted a monopoly for the slave trade with West Africa

1580–1640
Spanish rule of Portugal and Cape Verde

1620
Beginning of the salt trade on Sal and Maio

1680
Last eruption of the Pico Grande volcano on Fogo

Women squat on the roadside with baskets full of silvery fish, a group of men sit in the shade of a tree playing cards. Life here is leisurely and relaxed, people have time and they also have patience. The quiet serenity of the Cape Verdean people is remarkable, and this is despite the fact that life here is so hard that two-thirds of the population opt to live abroad.

EVERY ISLAND IS DIFFERENT

The name Cabo Verde – the green cape – is misleading as the archipelago in the Atlantic Ocean (600km off the west coast of Africa) is anything but green. The 4,033-km² group of 15 islands lies on the fringe of the Sahel zone and experiences extreme heat and aridity.

There is only sufficient water for agriculture on five of the nine inhabited islands – and that is only if the normal annual rainfall actually materialises. The other four islands are bone dry; brown deserts where the few solitary mountains are not able to halt the clouds brought by the constant north-easterly wind. The islands are categorised as being windward *(barlavento)* or leeward *(sotavento)* or by their geographic location: three flat, desert-like, eastern islands and the three-apiece mountainous northern and southern islands. Each island group, and each island, is different. The eastern islands of Sal, Boa Vista and Maio have magnificent white sandy beaches and are a paradise for water-sports enthusiasts. In the north there are Santo Antão and São Nicolau, with spectacular mountain panoramas and tropical valleys, while São Vicente is famous for Mindelo, its bustling port metropolis. The main islands in the south are Santiago,

1850-80
Mindelo booms as a hub for steam ship traffic

1967
The first hotel is opened in Santa Maria on Sal

1973
Freedom fighter Amílcar Cabral is murdered

1975
Political independence from Portugal

2014
Lava flows from the erupting Pico Pequeno on Fogo destroy two villages

2020/2021
Coronavirus brings tourism almost to a standstill

with the capital city, the almost 3,000m-high volcanic island of Fogo and the secluded, peaceful Brava.

From October to July, the north-east trade winds constantly blow over the islands, providing a pleasant, cooling breeze in the ever-present heat and creating heavenly conditions for windsurfers off the flat windward islands. The mountainous islands in the north benefit even more – because the mountains stop the clouds that the wind carries over the Atlantic, and the ensuing moisture keeps the north-eastern side of these islands green and fertile.

A MELTING POT

The first settlement on the formerly uninhabited islands was established in 1461 by seafarers sailing under the flag of the Portuguese king. Within a few decades as a Portuguese overseas colony, Cape Verde developed into the hub of the slave trade between Africa, Europe and America. White settlers from Europe came into contact with an increasing stream of slaves from Africa and their children formed the first generation of a new people: the Creoles. The customs and traditions of two continents produced a population with its characteristic culture and lifestyle. The Creole culture is colourful and full of vitality – in its emotional music, its dances and everyday customs. You will experience the exuberant joie de vivre of the carnival parades with beautiful dancers in magnificent feather costumes as well as at processions, religious festivals and family occasions.

The joy is infectious – so get involved (unless, of course, it's a private affair). **If someone gets a guitar and starts playing, stop and listen. If there is a dance, join in, and everybody will be delighted!**

INSIDER TIP Be part of it

A MODEL COUNTRY

Only around a third of Cape Verdeans are permanent residents on the islands – the rest live abroad, mainly in the United States, Portugal, France and West Africa. Many people perished from the repeated droughts and famines in the 1940s and many more were forced to emigrate so as not to starve.

Until a few years ago, the Cape Verde Islands were one of the poorest countries on earth. After 500 years of Portuguese exploitation, the country gained political independence in 1975. The independence pioneer was the Cape Verdean freedom fighter Amílcar Cabral. There has been a democratic, multi-party system in place since 1991, and Cape Verde is now a pluralist-parliamentary republic. A political and economic change has taken place in the last 35 years, one that has made it possible for the country to overcome hunger and poverty. Tourism plays an extremely important role, with the islands of Sal and Boa Vista attracting thousands of sun worshippers from Europe, while individual travellers often prefer the mountainous islands with their tourist infrastructure. Today, Cape Verde is regarded as a model in terms of democracy, politics and society among African countries.

AT A GLANCE

546,300
inhabitants

Canary Islands: 2,153,000

904 tons
CO_2 emissions annually/1,000 inhabitants

United Kingdom: 5,550 tons

119
landline connections/1,000 inhabitants

United Kingdom: 520

4,033km²
area

Canary Islands: 7,447km²

HIGHEST PEAK: PICO DO FOGO
2,829m

Ben Nevis: 1,345m

RAINY DAYS PER ANNUM
12

United Kingdom: 160

AVERAGE DAYTIME TEMPERATURE
27.1°C

United Kingdom: 13°C

In the Fragile States Index 2023, Cape Verde was the
THIRD
most stable nation in Africa

Only **12.7%**
of the population are married
United Kingdom: 50%

FAMOUS CAPE VERDEANS
Amílcar Cabral (politician)
Cesária Évora (singer)

FIRST-EVER COLONIAL SETTLEMENT IN THE TROPICS:
CIDADE VELHA

UNDERSTAND CAPE VERDE

ALUGUER

The *aluguer* (Portuguese: to rent) or *colectivo* is the most characteristic mode of transport in Cape Verde. These private vehicles with several seats travel between villages. Minibuses *(hiace)* are used for longer trips and open pickups with benches for shorter distances. The drivers pick up passengers at specific stops and also en route, and fares are officially regulated. If necessary, you will have to budge up to make room for new passengers – the vehicle is only full when there are 15 people on board … and drivers often only set off once all seats are occupied.

A STRONG FAITH

More than 80 per cent of Cape Verdeans are Catholics. This is no lip service; people actually live by their faith and don't just celebrate it in church. Many *aluguers* on Santiago display quotations on the windscreen or boot, such as "The Lord is my shepherd" or "May the Lord be with you" – and they mean it! There is a common response to "See you tomorrow": "*Se Deus quizer*" ("God willing"). Faith often requires strong commitment: in order to attend church services in rural areas, some people walk for miles.

Colectivo taxi on São Vicente

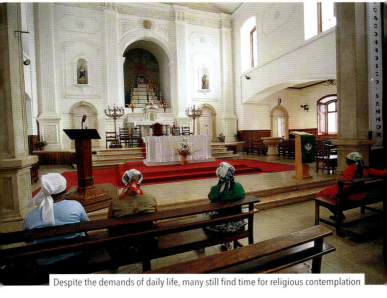

Despite the demands of daily life, many still find time for religious contemplation

RESPONSIBLE SPONSORING

Many families live hand to mouth and struggle to make ends meet. On the other hand, there are an increasing number of people who would like to share their relative wealth with the less fortunate. Here, it is important that help is directed to the right sources: as a tourist, rather than promoting begging in the streets, it is advisable to support one of the country's recognised charities.

MERCEARIA & BARBEARIA

The general store and the barber – there is one of each in every village. You will find an inconspicuous *mercearia* that sells just about everything and also acts as a bar on almost every street corner. As one customer buys a bag of flour, a tablespoon of paprika or a couple of stock cubes, so another one lifts his glass of *grogue* to toast all those present. The *barbearia*, where men not only go for a haircut but also a shave, is often a little harder to find – pop your head through an open door and you may well find a customer sat upon an often-ancient barber's chair, probably dating from the 1960s or 1970s.

BRAIDS

Regardless of sex or age, many men, women and children have their hair woven into small braids *(tranças)*. There is an endless variety of hairstyles, and if the locals get tired of their style after a few days, they simply have a new one done. The ends of the braids are usually decorated with colourful plastic beads.

SODADE

For the Cape Verdeans, *sodade* refers to the sense of irretrievable loss and unquenchable longing – for the distant homeland, a lost love, the family or the past. This bittersweet longing finds its main expression in melancholic *morna* songs.

WATER

Nothing is more precious than water in Cape Verde. None of the islands has sufficient rainfall, and the cisterns that can be seen everywhere have to be filled by tank trucks most of the time. In rural areas, water has to be collected from public outlets and taken home in plastic canisters on the back of a donkey. Modern hotels have their own desalination plants. Do your bit and save as much water as you can.

RABELADOS

Rabelados is a term that refers to the members of an ethnic group on Santiago, whose historical roots lie in groups of escaped slaves. They protected themselves from re-capture with a sophisticated behavioural code: living well hidden in remote areas, taking neither food nor drinks from external parties, never divulging their name, etc. In the 1940s, the *rabelados* completely excluded themselves from

You will hear music almost everywhere on Cape Verde, and it's often live

society for religious and political reasons. It wasn't until half a century later that the Cape Verdean artist Misá broke with the isolation and created a new form of artistic expression in the 1990s. Since then the community, which follows its own rules, has increasingly opened up to external influences. Now, visitors are even welcome in their biggest village of Espinho Branco. Here they can get an impression of the *rabelados*' lifestyle and perhaps even take something away with them. One thing is for sure: it will be a unique experience.

DIZZYING

Music is everywhere in Cape Verde, either the Cape Verdean version of American pop, with Caribbean, Brazilian and African influences, or the traditional *coladeira*, *morna* or *funana*. The Cape Verdeans love to dance, especially the lively, free *coladeira* and the rhythmical dance to *funana* music. You will hardly find a man here who won't enthusiastically take his partner to the dance floor, where legs and hips are swung in a dizzying manner! And the women-only *batuco* is equally lively. However, there is also the melancholic *morna*, made known by Cape Verde's most famous musician: *morna* performer Cesária Évora (1947–2011), who started life as a girl from a poor family in Mindelo and eventually caught the world's attention, aged 47. Throughout her entire life she performed barefoot to demonstrate her solidarity with the poor and homeless in her country.

TRUE OR FALSE?

CABO VERDE – THE GREEN CAPE

This is how the name translates. However, the country is anything but green. Brown, yes, all shades of brown or even yellow (due to the dry vegetation), but certainly not green – at least in most places and most of the time. Some areas in Cape Verde don't see rain for several years. The rest of the archipelago turns green after the rainy season, but the drought often returns within a few weeks. Lush places, such as Ribeira do Paúl (Santo Antão), where the vegetation is verdant all year round, are few and far between. The real green cape, after which Cape Verde was originally named, is 600km to the east in Senegal.

MUSIC IN THE BLOOD

Are all Cape Verdeans potential musicians and do they perform on every street corner? Well, almost. People here have rhythm in their blood, and even self-declared non-dancers among the locals make the average European look positively stiff. However, while loud music may keep you awake on certain nights, even the cultural capital Mindelo may disappoint music lovers if they look for live events at the wrong time. And the likes of Neúza, Mayra Andrade or Lura, once up-and-coming local musicians, are now internationally renowned stars.

Grogue production: first, the juice is extracted from the sugar cane using a press

EXCUSE ME?

The national language in Cape Verde is Kriolu: a varied mixture of African and European influences (mainly Portuguese). Having originated in the age of the Portuguese discoveries and the slave trade, this language has remained alive and has continued to develop. On São Vicente, for example, you find many English words; on Boa Vista there are Jewish linguistic roots; on Santiago the greatest number of African expressions; and on Santo Antão many French terms. Every island has its own variations: for example, on Santiago "let's go" is *nubai!* on Fogo it's *dubai!* on São Vicente it's *nobai!* and on Santo Antão it's *nobé!* It is unsurprising that the people have struggled to agree on a single common version so that Kriolu can become a written language and the official language of Cape Verde. For the time being the official language remains Portuguese – in the media, at school and for official business.

SCHOOL

Do not be surprised if you happen to see school-aged children walking around in the mornings. The primary school system on Cape Verde works on a shift pattern. One group of children is taught from 8am to 12.30pm, then all the pupils have their lunch together and between 1pm and 5.30pm the second group of children has its turn. School is only mandatory up until Year 6. If you want your children to have further education, you will have to pay for that yourself.

SLAVE TRADE

Two factors set a chain of events in motion in the second half of the 15th century: Spain and Portugal colonised Africa and America and a new foodstuff became fashionable in Europe – sugar. The sugar cane plantations in the colonies were worked by slaves who were transported from the western coast of Africa in their thousands. Within just a few decades, a profitable three-way trade that cost millions of people their life came into being: weapons and manufactured goods went to Africa, slaves to America and sugar and rum to Europe. Its location made Cape Verde an important hub, and Ribeira Grande rapidly developed into one of the most important trading centres of the slave trade. The booming business with human lives brought unimaginable wealth to European dynasties and privateers, and went on until the 1850s before finally being abolished.

CAPE VERDE PATCHWORK

If Ineida is the sister of José and Aldina, and the mother of Joana and Arlinda, while José is the brother of Joana, Rui and António, but not of Arlinda, and Arlinda's siblings are Maria, Nelson, Jailson and Manuel, then you have a … Cape Verde patchwork. Family ties are complicated and intricate. Half-siblings as well as numerous cousins, nieces, great-nephews, aunts or great-uncles from other branches of the family are the rule, not the exception. However, the current social and economical development of the country has brought a trend towards increased family planning. Women have become more independent and are more able to look after themselves without the need for a male provider for themselves and their children. While fathers are in theory liable for maintenance, in practice mothers often have to care for their offspring on their own.

GROGUE

Sugar cane everywhere, at least on the four mountainous islands of Santiago, Brava, Santo Antão and São Nicolau. The Portuguese colonialists planted sugar cane and cotton and soon started trading in them. Until the beginning of the 18th century the entire sugar cane harvest was exported, then the farmers on Santo Antão started using it to distil rum (Creole: *grogue*). They used mobile sugar cane presses to extract the juice from the cane and then let it ferment in open barrels before distilling in large copper kilns. The freshly distilled clear liquor is known as *grogue novo* (new rum); after a minimum of three years of aging in a wooden barrel, this matures to *grogue velha* (old rum) which is light brown and far gentler and milder than the original firewater. *Grogue* becomes *pontche* when it is mixed with sugar cane molasses, and when mixed with sugar and fruit, it turns into liqueur – coconut, mango, passion fruit, lemon, tamarind, etc. *Grogue* has an alcohol content of around 40 per cent and is produced on all of the mountainous islands, but it is said that the best comes from Santo Antão.

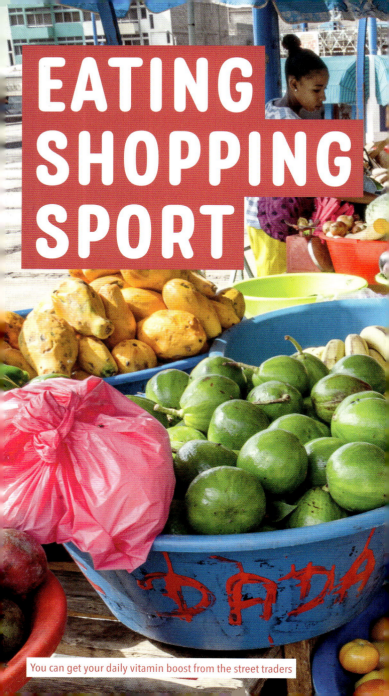

EATING SHOPPING SPORT

You can get your daily vitamin boost from the street traders

EATING & DRINKING

The food served in Cape Verde depends entirely on the means. When the family comes together, often including relatives and friends, poverty and wealth are mirrored on the dinner plate: maize and beans for some, probably with vegetables, and a piece of fish, meat and lobster for others.

ALL KINDS OF STEW

Cachupa is the national dish of Cape Verde, a stew of sweetcorn, beans and vegetables that is refined with meat, sausage or fish – if available. The ubiquitous *cachupa* is served first as a thick soup and then the next morning it is fried with onions and possibly an egg, and eaten for breakfast. It is far more than just a nourishing meal – it is an essential part of the Cape Verdean lifestyle and an important aspect of the country's national identity.

GOURMET HITS FRESH FROM THE SEA

Fish *(pexi)* is also frequently eaten. There are many varieties available from the surrounding ocean: small fish such as *garoupa*, *cavala* and *bonito* are prepared whole, complete with head and bones; larger fish such as *serra*, *dorada*, *esmoregal* and tuna *(atum)* are served as fillets – usually grilled. *Seafood* such as squid, mussels and other shellfish are always fresh and prepared in a variety of tasty ways. However, you should forgo the highly sought-after lobster during the closed season from July to November.

MEAT? FISH!

The fresh fish in Cape Verde is hard to beat and definitely preferable to meat *(kárni)* – especially if the chicken *(frángu)* comes from the deep freeze and not the cook's own farm. The increasing use of frozen foods on the

Typical for Cape Verde are *cachupa* (left) and banana bread with coffee (right)

islands is a questionable matter (and can even be dangerous) as there is little guarantee that there has not been a power cut in Cape Verde. You should also be wary of pork as there is no trichinella inspection programme, or anything similar, on some of the islands. Beef is usually not a problem, but it can be quite tough.

On the other hand, there are plenty of vegetables prepared in a variety of ways. They are normally served as side dishes to go with meat or fish, because few restaurants cater for vegetarians or vegans. However, on request *(sem carne, sem peixe)* most chefs will make you an omelette or a pasta or vegetable dish. Be prepared for a mixture of sweet potato, carrots, manioc and *inhame* (taro), breadfruit, pumpkin, cabbage, potatoes, etc. – depending on the season. To be on the safe side, tell them that you don't want to eat ham *(fiambre)* or sausage meats *(chouriço)*.

SWEET & SAVOURY

For dessert a pudding is often on the menu: *pudim de leite* (milk), *coco* (coconut) or *queijo* (goat's milk), as well as fresh fruit. Papayas and bananas are harvested throughout the year, while mangos, guavas, *pinha* (custard apple), passion fruit, coconuts, apples, as well as pomegranates from Fogo, figs and quinces are only available in season. The best-known dessert is *doce de papaya com queijo* – candied slices of papaya with spicy goat's cheese – called "*Romeo e Julia*". The goat's cheese from Fogo and Santo Antão is renowned in Cape Verde for its fine taste and quality.

LOVELY DRINKS

The coffee *(kafé)* from Fogo, as well as the wine produced on the island

Also delicious as a dessert: goat's cheese, best sourced from Fogo or Santo Antão

(vinho de Fogo), has a unique taste thanks to the volcanic soil that gives the beans and grapes a full, fruity flavour. As well as the long-established wine brands Chã and Sodade, there is the more recent Vinha Maria Chaves, introduced in 2005 by Italian Capuchin monks. Apart from Fogo, wine is only grown on Santo Antão – for private consumption. Here, as well as on the neighbouring island of São Nicolau and on Santiago, coffee bushes of the *Arabica* variety grow at altitudes between 660m and 800m. In the cool uplands the coffee beans mature slowly, developing their wonderful aroma.

All of the mountainous Cape Verde islands produce the traditional island drink of *grogue* (sugar cane rum). A dash of bitter-sweet sugar cane syrup *(mel)* turns *grogue* into *pontche,* the traditional sugar cane liqueur. Liqueurs that are made with fruit, herbs or nuts are often called *caipirinha.* Strela, the local beer *(serveja),* is brewed in Praia, the capital city, but most Cape Verdeans prefer beer imported from Portugal. Don't drink the tap water – buy bottled water instead. Ice cubes are not always safe either, and cocktails and soft drinks with ice can be a bit risky.

EAT LIKE THE LOCALS

There are plenty of local restaurants that serve simple, regional food. A *cachupa* is a standard dish in most of them and this is a good sign because it means that the locals eat there! It is a good idea to ask for the dish of the day *(prato do dia)* at lunchtime – it is always freshly prepared and usually inexpensive. Stews, fish and chicken are the most common dishes.

Most restaurants are open from midday to 3pm and from 6/7pm to 10/11pm. Cafés are usually open all day long. You might go unnoticed if you sit down at an outside table so, to avoid waiting too long, it is best to go inside to place your order.

Today's Menu

Aperitivo

CAIPIRINHA DE GROGUE
A version of the Brazilian national drink using *grogue*

Entrada

QUEIJO DE CABRA GRELHADO COM MEL DE CANA
Grilled goat's milk cream cheese with sugar cane syrup

CANJA DE GALINHA
Chicken soup with rice and vegetables

BÚZIO ESTUFADO
Whelks braised in tomatoes and onions

Prato principal

BIFE DE ATUM
Tuna steak with rice, vegetables and chips

FRANGO ASSADO
Grilled chicken with chips or rice and vegetables

FEIJOADA
Hearty bean stew with vegetables, bacon and meat

ESTUFADA DE CABRITO
Goat kid casserole with vegetables

GAROUPA GRELHADO COM ARROZ E LEGUMES
Grilled perch with rice and vegetables

ESPARGUETE DE MARISCO
Spaghetti with mixed seafood

Sobremesa

PUDIM DE QUEIJO
A goat's cheese dessert (pudding)

ROMEO E JULIA
Fresh goat's cheese with glacéed papaya

BANANA FLAMBÉ
Banana flambéed with *grogue*

Digestivo

GROGUE VELHA
Sugar cane liqueur matured in wooden casks

PONCHE DE MEL
Liqueur made from sugar cane spirit, sugar cane syrup and lime

SHOPPING

GROWN ON A VOLCANO

The only main wine-growing region is Fogo, where the *vinho de Fogo* is stored in three vintners' vaults. The best is Chã das Caldeiras. Its grapes grow in the volcano's *caldeira*, and it is delicious and reasonably priced. Sodade is grown on the western mountainside. Vinha Maria Chaves is pressed on the left-hand side of the road shortly after São Filipe. *Manecom* is self-pressed house wine and is of varying quality.

A GOOD STRATEGY

Counting continuously, coming up with tactics, setting traps, only to be outwitted by your opponent in the end? *Oril requires nothing more than a wooden plank* with six indentations on each side and 48 tokens made of dried seeds of the *Orileira* bush.

Take an *Oril* game home with you and play an analogue game for a change! It is bound to entertain you and your cunning opponent for some time.

TASTY SOUVENIRS

If you like edible souvenirs, visit one of the local cooperatives: jams and liqueurs, dried fruit and herbs, goat's milk yoghurt and cheese, coffee, etc. Delicious! Try Fogo coffee as a souvenir: it's a rarity even among true aficionados.

INSIDER TIP
Rare beans

PANOS

Panos are narrow woven strips of cotton that are usually worn around the hips or as a strap for carrying babies. During the age of the slave trade they were used as currency. Traditional black and white *panos* with geometric patterns are made on Santiago and Fogo, but there are also modern, colourful variants.

There is always space in your suitcase for a colourful *pano* or a bag of coffee

FLUFFY DASHBOARD COVERS

Since summers are getting hotter, car dashboards may soon need to be protected from the bleaching sunlight! In many *aluguers* you can see colourful mini-flokatis which combine sun protection and a youthful design. They are available in markets and numerous small shops.

AFRICAN PATTERN MIXTURE

Colourful printed fabrics with marvellous patterns from Senegal can be turned into clothing, curtains, tablecloths and many other beautiful and useful items. There are a few young female designers who make these colourful pieces by hand, for example Wanda Fernandes on Boa Vista and Swiss-born Franziska Brodbeck on Santo Antão.

FASHIONABLE UPCYCLING

Beautiful items are given a new lease of life: empty juice containers are turned into bags, bottle tops into earrings, rolled newspaper into lampshades and old toothbrushes into funny figurines. Multi-coloured toys created from discarded metal cans have always been a part of childhood in Cape Verde. Also unique are handbags, bracelets, etc. made from old tyre tubes.

SPORT & ACTIVITIES

If you love an active holiday, Cape Verde is great for hiking, climbing, mountain biking, kayaking and canyoning, paragliding, stand-up paddling, fishing, snorkelling and diving, surfing and sailing!

DIVING

The ocean flora and fauna in Cape Verde are extremely varied. When diving, you will encounter huge and colourful schools of fish, turtles and, with a bit of luck, larger fish such as rays, wahoos, barracudas or nurse sharks. Due to the isolated location of the archipelago, it is possible to discover endemic species such as Cape Verde black seabream, sea snails and the Cape demoiselle, a funny looking kind of damselfish. Even in winter, water temperatures don't drop below 20°C, and in late summer the thermometer can indicate 27°C. The location of the islands and the steady winds can produce demanding waves and currents. The sea is at its calmest during the summer months of July and August.

The sea around Sal offers more than two dozen interesting dive sites with a breathtaking variety of species and diverse characteristics including wrecks and caves. Directly off the picture-postcard beach of Santa Maria are 10–40m-deep dive sites with visibilities of more than 20m. Boa Vista offers an equally rich fauna, but the dive sites are further out and there is often a strong swell with churned-up sand. In Tarrafal on Santiago the rocky ocean floor usually ensures better visibility, and at Porto Novo and Tarrafal on Santo Antão you can explore other wonderful dive sites.

FISHING

Whether you are a beginner or a professional, everybody can enjoy fishing

in Cape Verde and will catch something on one of the tourist boats or while out at sea with one the local fishermen. Copy the locals: tie a stone to the end of the line as a weight and fix some bait to a hook a few inches higher up. Then lower the line in the right spot and be prepared to react quickly if a fish takes the bait. From blue-spotted groupers to the respect-demanding moray eel – all kinds of fish can be caught. Just be aware that the boats are small, you may get seasick and the sun is even stronger than on land.

FOOTBALL

If you like to play football, you can explore a new version here: pack a ball and a pump in your suitcase (which you can give away before returning home) and turn up at the football pitch (even the

smallest village will have one), and very quickly two teams will face each other. Football is *the* national sport in Cape Verde, and people kick a ball around on all the islands even in the most remote hamlets. Most of the boys and an increasing number of girls join in, and every larger festival also includes a football tournament lasting several days. The final of the island championships is a big annual event, and even the ferry schedules may be changed at short notice to accommodate it.

HIKING

The demanding walks will be worth it when you get to enjoy fabulous views of the agricultural terraces and water channels (*levadas*) in inaccessible gorges that were created hundreds of years ago, with the azure sea in the background. Ancient, cobbled donkey tracks connect villages, which are spectacularly huddled into the landscape, and are ideal for hiking. Most certainly you will hear a friendly *"Bom dia!"* along the way. And don't be surprised if the villagers invite you to rest in the shade for a little while. They are used to the mercilessly hot sun and ask themselves why anybody would want to voluntarily climb the mountains in the midday sun for no obvious reason ... Good sun protection, proper hiking boots and a sufficient water supply are essential to hike safely in Cape Verde, as well as a sound sense of direction. There are some hikes, e.g. in the highlands of Santo Antão, which you should not attempt without a knowledgeable local guide.

PARAGLIDING

Let paragliding instructor Emi *(tel. 9 10 20 10 | altitude.cv)* take you on a tandem trip up above your favourite island. The likeable and professional paraglider fell in love with the archipelago only a few years ago. You will make use of the thermals, rise up to the skies and enjoy the wonderful landscape from a bird's eye view. Flights are possible from seven of the nine inhabited islands, including over the moon-like landscape of Chã das Caldeiras on Fogo.

INSIDER TIP
Soar with ospreys

SAILING

The sea and air temperature is never below 20°C, there's always a decent wind and crystal-clear water with whales and turtles, and even flying fish that land on your deck just in time for dinner. Pristine beaches and demanding nautical challenges make a sailor's happiness complete. Winds of up to force 8 on the Beaufort scale are not uncommon from November to April; they are not quite as strong in summer. The only yacht harbour in Cape Verde is in Mindelo, and if you don't have your own boat, you can charter a yacht or book a trip with a crew.

SNORKELLING

The strong surf and unpredictable currents mean that snorkelling is only possible in sheltered areas off the coast of the mountainous islands, such as in the bays of Tarrafal/Santiago and Tarrafal de Monte Trigo/Santo

Antão or the Baía das Gatas on São Vicente. How about seeing eye to eye with the world's biggest fish? Off Boa Vista, from July to December, with a bit of luck you can encounter whale sharks or rays!

SURFING

Classic surfing is especially popular on Sal. It is also possible off Santiago and São Vicente, while Santo Antão is preferred by bodyboarders. Excellent for kite- and windsurfing are Sal, Boa Vista and São Vicente.

In recent years, Cape Verde has developed into a kitesurfing centre. At the beginning of the year, the GKA Kitesurf World Cup takes off here. Josh Angulo, a former windsurfing world champion who grew up in a Hawaiian surfing family, has chosen Santa Maria as his new base. The Sal-born Mitu Monteiro, former kite-surfing world champion, started surfing without foot straps because he couldn't afford them. And the island continues to produce top surfers. The reasons are to be found in the north-east trade winds as well as the large variety of suitable spots for both beginners (Costa da Fragata) and pros (Ponta Preta). Although the winds vary throughout the year, they are extremely reliable, especially from November to June. The strongest surf occurs between January and March. For information, please look online, e.g. at *capeverdeislands.org/surfing-sal* (wind, kite) and *surfinn.travel/best-surfspots-capeverde* (surfing).

Cape Verde kitesurfers don't have to wait long for the perfect wave

REGIONAL
OVERVIEW

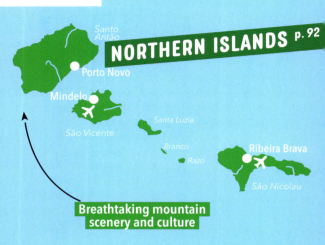

Santo Antão

NORTHERN ISLANDS p. 92

Porto Novo

Mindelo

São Vicente

Santa Luzia

Branco

Razo

Ribeira Brava

São Nicolau

Breathtaking mountain scenery and culture

$O \quad C \quad E \quad A \quad N \quad O$

$A \quad T \quad L \quad \hat{A} \quad N \quad T \quad I \quad C \quad O$

History, volcanoes and tropical plants

SOUTHERN ISLANDS p. 66

Fogo

Ilhéus Secos ou do Rombo

Brava

São Filipe

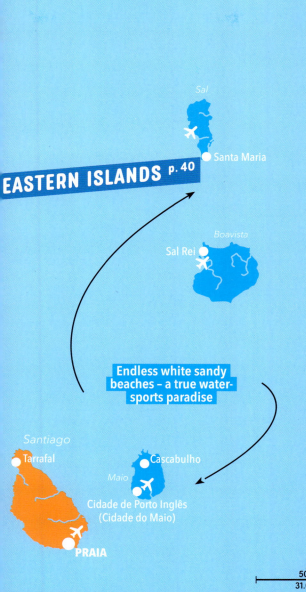

Sal

✈

● Santa Maria

EASTERN ISLANDS P. 40

Boavista

Sal Rei ●✈

Endless white sandy beaches – a true water-sports paradise

Santiago

○ Tarrafal

● Cascabulho

Maio

✈

Cidade de Porto Inglês
(Cidade do Maio)

✈

● **PRAIA**

▲

50 km
31.07 mi

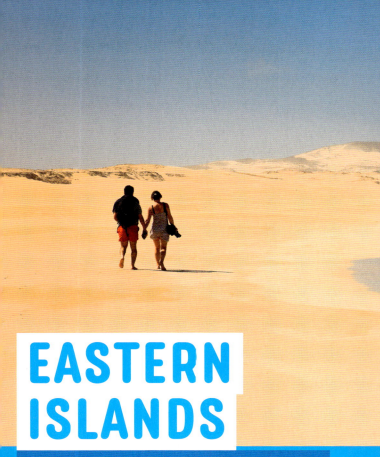

EASTERN ISLANDS

The air is dusty and dry, the fine sand blows into your ears and eyes – the three islands of Sal, Boa Vista and Maio are known as the "desert islands" and the name suits them to a tee.

There is plenty of desert here – endless reddish-brown fields of stone without any vegetation, where the occasional acacia bush rises from the barren soil, and dazzling white dunes formed from sand that has been carried here from the Sahara. It is amazing to see how the dry steppes and barren salt marshes gradually turn into the most

Sandy beaches and dunes stretching for miles: Praia da Chave on Boa Vista

wonderful beaches on the coast: miles of fine white sand and dazzling, crystal-clear turquoise water that will fulfil all your holiday dreams.

The eastern islands are especially popular with water-sports enthusiasts, as they boast the perfect conditions for wind- and kitesurfing, surfing, sailing, diving, snorkelling and fishing. Ornithologists and other nature lovers will also find plenty to interest them as they can observe ospreys and tropical seabirds as well as the sea turtles that come on shore on summer nights to lay their eggs in the warm sand.

EASTERN ISLANDS

MARCO POLO HIGHLIGHTS

★ **PEDRA DE LUME**
Swimmers can float in the buoyant salt-pan waters ➤ p. 45

★ **PRAIA DE SANTA MARIA**
Surfing, sunbathing and swimming: a dream for water-sports enthusiasts ➤ p. 50

★ **DESERTO DE VIANA**
An endless chain of dunes – all the way to the horizon ➤ p. 54

★ **PRAIA DA VARANDINHA**
An off-road trip to the perfect beach ➤ p. 58

★ **CIDADE DE PORTO INGLÊS**
Where life moves at a slow and deeply relaxing pace ➤ p. 61

★ **PRAIA DE SANTANA**
A beach with 25m-high dunes of fine Sahara sand ➤ p. 65

OCEANO
ATLÂNTICO

Praia de Santana ★

Cascabulho

Morrinho

14 Acacia forests

Pedro Vaz

Calheta **15**

Maio
p. 60

Alcatraz
Pilão Cão

2½ hrs

14 Acacia forests

13 Morro

Figueira da Horta

Saltworks **12**

Praia do Porto Inglês

11 Cidade de
Porto Inglês ★

16 Ribeira Dom João

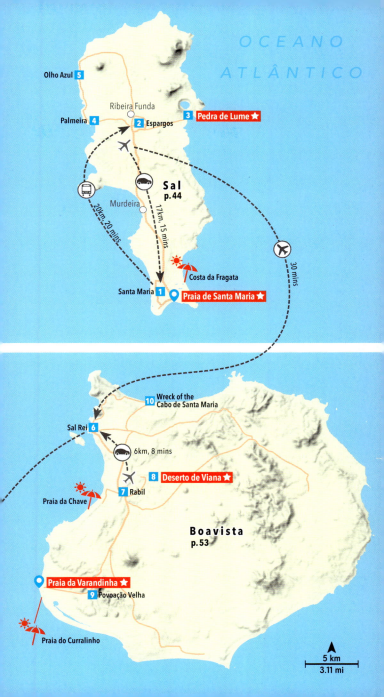

OCEANO ATLÂNTICO

Olho Azul **5**

Ribeira Funda

Palmeira **4**

2 Espargos

3 **Pedra de Lume** ★

Sal p.44

Murdeira

20km, 20 mins

17km, 15 mins

Costa da Fragata

Santa Maria **1**

Praia de Santa Maria ★

30 mins

10 Wreck of the Cabo de Santa Maria

Sal Rei **6**

6km, 8 mins

8 **Deserto de Viana** ★

Praia da Chave

7 Rabil

Boavista p.53

Praia da Varandinha ★

9 Povoação Velha

Praia do Curralinho

5 km
3.11 mi

SAL

(🗺 Q–R 4–6) **Measuring 30km from north to south and 12km from west to east, Sal (pop. 38,000) is the most north-easterly island in the archipelago and the flattest of all.**

As soon as you arrive, you will see what the island is all about: extensive areas of sand and stone in all shades of brown, dotted with acacia bushes shaped by the wind which has decorated their branches with colourful plastic bags. Heading south, the stony desert turns into a light-brown landscape of dunes with white picture-postcard beaches stretching for miles: the main attraction! Santa Maria, the Cape Verde tourist showpiece, is reached on the island's only tarmacked road.

The island's highest points are Monte Leste (263m) and Monte Grande (406m). Both are part of a volcanic chain in the rugged north of the island. Just a few dozen people live here, and the only signs of life are a few solitary goats wandering freely across the stony fields. Visible from the airport is the island's capital Espargos. On the west coast, the rocks of Buracona tempt tourists to go on an excursion, while the east coast offers the salt works at Pedra de Lume.

SIGHTSEEING

1 SANTA MARIA

Santa Maria is a small town (pop. 6,500) that owes its existence to salt. It was founded by a Portuguese trader in 1830 in order to exploit the extensive salt flats. Not much is left from those days: a wooden windmill in front of the Hotel Morabeza and the restored weighing house by the fishermen's pier, which is an attraction in itself – around lunchtime the local fishermen return from the sea and land their catch here. It is amazing to see what creatures live in the ocean – there will almost certainly be a species that you haven't seen before! Some of the fish are gutted and cut up immediately, while others are sold whole. The historic *weighing house* is the place where the salt used to be weighed before it was loaded on to the ships.

Nowadays, tourism has become the most important economic activity. Most holidaymakers stay in the hotel district to the west of the old harbour quay that runs for a few miles along the beach. There are beach clubs run by the hotels, restaurants, surf stations and diving schools along the entire length of the beach promenade. During the day there is plenty of action here, but in the evening the small alleyways surrounding the main square become more interesting: countless souvenir shops, bars and restaurants provide entertainment for all tastes.

The town centre consists of the main square – the Praça Marcelo Leitão – with the Catholic church and the three adjacent parallel streets: Rua Amílcar Cabral, Rua 1 de Junho and Rua 15 de Agosto. The one- and two-storey houses in various stages of dilapidation and a few manor houses in the Portuguese colonial style create

The once-valuable salt mined near Pedra de Lume gave Sal its name

a fascinating contrast to the modern shops.

Nice for a break is the small, quiet and picturesque 🐾 🌡 *Viveiro Eco Park (daily 10am–6pm | admission 5 euros, children up to 5 free | EuroZona da Fatima | FB: viveirocaboverde)*, where you can find a shady spot between lush plants and animal enclosures. It's great for watching, strolling, relaxing and just slowing down. There's also a mini petting zoo, which is great for families. 🔲 *R6*

2 ESPARGOS

The island's capital (pop. 22,000) at the foot of *Monte Curral* is 2km from the airport. The cube-shaped houses in pastel shades of blue, yellow and pink look European until you spot the colourfully dressed women selling bananas, papayas and fresh fish in bright plastic bowls on the side of the road. European? African? A bit of everything. The men gather to play 🚩 *oril* under the trees while the Praça 5 de Julho in the centre appears drowsy. Here you can visit the turquoise *Nazarene church*, and most of the town's guesthouses and restaurants are also nearby. 🔲 *R5*

3 PEDRA DE LUME ⭐

The salt works near the hamlet of Pedra de Lume (pop. 400) are 6km from Espargos. Salt production was once the economic engine of the entire island. A 1km-wide natural crater, with its base below sea level, offered perfect conditions for the salt trade. The salt works were in commercial use from 1805 when wind

You're in the middle of the action in Santa Maria's roadside bars

turbines and pumps were installed, and at its peak it employed several hundred workers. A tunnel was bored through the crater wall and from 1919 a cable car was used to transport salt to the port, 1km away. Salt was exported from Pedra de Lume to Latin America and Africa until the 1930s; after that the salt works lost their importance. Today, only a handful of fishermen live in Pedra de Lume but the salt works are a great tourist attraction. Take a dip in one of the salt pans – it is the same as in the Dead Sea – you cannot sink!

The *salinas* are also of interest to naturalists because they are home to many migratory birds and local species. The best time to visit is the afternoon when the salt pans shimmer in myriad hues of pink and violet. Photographers love the wooden supports of the cable, the slowly degrading, historic salt-loading station and the rusty barges in the small harbour which provide bizarre picture opportunities. *R5*

4 PALMEIRA

The former fishing village of Palmeira (pop. 1,400) has become the main hub for everything that reaches the island by ship. Oil tankers and container ships unload their cargo next to colourful fishing boats. The

rock pools. In stormy conditions, bathing is not allowed, but you still get an impressive spectacle of nature with the awesome spray and thundering swell. *From Palmeira take the coastal road, direction north, for approx. 6km |* 🗺 *Q4*

EATING & DRINKING

ANGULO BEACH CLUB
The location is a dream and the atmosphere is relaxed. During the day you can admire the daredevil surfers and the magnificent views, while in the evening enjoy the sunset on the beach and the fact that you are lucky enough to be on holiday here. *Daily | Santa Maria | Praia Antonio Sousa | tel. 2 42 15 80 | €€*

ATLANTIS
In 2016, the Atlantis burnt down completely, but by February 2020 proprietor Patrik had managed to rebuild it. Thank you, Patrik! The new restaurant has a similar airy and rustic ambience and divine sea views. Its French-and-Creole cuisine is second to none. *Daily | Santa Maria | beach promenade opposite the Hotel Belorizonte | tel. 9 91 28 57 | €€*

CAPE FRUIT
The atmosphere here – thanks to colourful cushions, hammocks, brightly painted furniture and the many plants – has a tropical vibe, which goes well with the fruit that is served. Banana, mango, passionfruit, papaya, guava, etc. come as a salad, smoothie or ice cream, on crêpes and with yoghurt, as

up-and-coming harbour town is becoming increasingly important for the island and not much remains of what was once a picturesque port.

5 OLHO AZUL
Near Buracona on the north-west coast, the sea has carved a deep hole out of the volcanic rock: the *Olho Azul*. Here, when the sun is at the right angle (approx. 11am–1pm), the water sparkles in incredible shades of blue. Unfortunately, the crowds of tourists have increased to an extent that you have to wait your turn to gaze into the deep blue. If the weather is reasonably calm, you can bathe in the adjacent

jams, freshly pressed juice and more. *Thu–Tue | Santa Maria | Rua 15 de Agosto | tel. 9 82 22 05 | FB | €€*

CHEZ PASTIS

Herbert and his team enjoy a superb reputation so booking is essential. You can look forward to culinary delights such as "fish fantasy" or a first-class steak and more. *Daily | Santa Maria | Rua Amílcar Cabral 5 | tel. 9 84 36 96 | FB | €€€*

O FAROLIM

The restaurant in the Hotel Odjo d'Água has a truly magical setting above the sea. The sound of the surf, Cape Verde songs and an exquisite meal – it's the most beautiful place on the island for a romantic dinner. And it's not exclusively for hotel guests. *Daily | Santa Maria | in the Odjo d'Água hotel complex | tel. 2 42 14 14 | €€€*

LEONARDO

Fine Italian delicacies in friendly surroundings. Alessandro the proprietor serves tasty meat dishes, fresh fish, home-made pasta and a superb selection of international wines to go with the food. Treat yourself! *Daily | Santa Maria | centre | tel. 9 81 00 57 | FB: leonardocafecapoverde | €€€*

MAREA

INSIDER TIP
Italian & homemade

You can find homemade bread and pasta at Franca and Davide's from Italy! However, in order to enjoy these and other delicacies, you first need to book a table and then manage to find

the right address ... but it will be worth the effort! *Closed Sun | Santa Maria | Rua de Salinas | tel. 9 82 21 65 | €€–€€€*

SHOPPING

L'ALAMBIC

"100% Cape Verdean" is the slogan for this tiny shop. No imported goods – only locally produced items. This applies to the *grogue* and the homemade liqueurs (please taste them!), as well as the coffee, wine, salt, etc. *Santa Maria | Les Alizés ground floor | FB: lalambiccaboverde*

DJUNTA MO ART

Another shop that sells exclusively Cape Verdean arts and crafts. Textiles, original bags and other accessories, jewellery, local and regional specialties – handmade souvenirs instead of mass-produced items. *Santa Maria | Rua 1 de Junho | FB*

SPORT & ACTIVITIES

RIDING

Fly along the white beaches on horseback, with the sea breeze in your hair, feeling free and unrestricted ... This should engage all horse lovers, but even first-timers will enjoy horse riding on the island. At

INSIDER TIP
Safely in the saddle

Santa Marilha Horse Excursions both beginners and children are secure in the saddle – thanks to their excellent safety and service and friendly support *(Santa Maria | tel. 5 89 81 21 | horseexcursionsal.com).*

TURTLE WATCHING

Experience the wonders of nature at close range, either on a walk between July and October, when the turtles (up to 1.20m long) lay their eggs in the sand at night, or during a visit to the turtle baby protection station of the charitable *Project Biodiversity (donations welcome | projectbiodiversity. org)* between September and December. Either way, it's a fascinating and wonderful experience.

WATER SPORTS

Dozens of colourful kites sail through the air, courageous kiters speed across the water on their boards, performing metre-high jumps... Experienced kite surfers have fun at *Ponta Preta* and along the west coast, whereas beginners are advised to stay with the onshore winds at the *Praia da Fragata*.

Sal is regarded among windsurfers as one of the world's hotspots. They enjoy the speed tracks and long swell as well as steep surf waves in the *Leme Bedje* surf area. At the *Ponta Preta* World Cup spot, 3–4m-high waves break in the immediate vicinity of the rocky lava shore: only recommended for pros! Beginners are better off at the *Praia de Santa Maria* and the *Praia Antonio Sousa*. Naturally, the surf station of former World Champion Josh Angulo *(Angulo Cabo Verde Windsurf Center | Santa Maria | tel. 2 42 15 80 | angulocaboverde.com)* has only the very best equipment. Depending on the wind and waves, you will be given the optimum kit for surfing, kite- and windsurfing or stand-up paddleboarding.

Final preparations at Ponta Preta before riding the waves

Divers will also find good conditions on Sal. Visit *Cabo Verde Diving (tel. 9 97 88 24 | FB)* and *Eco Dive School Cabo Verde (tel. 9 81 92 87 | FB)* to enjoy incredible underwater adventures.

BEACHES

A chain of perfect beaches starts at *Praia de Santa Maria* and makes its way as far as *Baía de Algodoeiro*. However, there is no shade at all and you'll only find umbrellas at the places that cater to tourists. If you are planning to spread out your beach towel anywhere else, make sure you take everything with you, including proper sunburn protection and bottles of water.

BAÍA DE MURDEIRA

Murdeira is on the west coast around 6km south of Espargos. There is a smaller cove in the long bay and it is perfect for bathing. A holiday complex with apartments and restaurants provides the perfect infrastructure not only for a beach break but also for day guests. *R5*

COSTA DA FRAGATA

A desert track on the south-east coast about 3km north of Santa Maria leads to the Costa da Fragata. The 4km-long beach is not particularly wide but it is very popular with kite surfers and generally known as "Kite Beach". *R6*

PONTA PRETA

The rocky promontory of Ponta Preta is in the south-west, around 2km from

Santa Maria. It owes its fame to several windsurfing world championships, but this surf spot is only suitable for real experts! Watch them display their incredible skills at close range. *R6*

PRAIA DE SANTA MARIA

The island's main beach stretches 9km from Ponta do Sinó to Ponta Preta. The hotels, beach bars and clubs create a holiday atmosphere and there are surf and diving bases that offer all kinds of water sports. *R6*

WELLNESS

BEAUTY PLAZA

Treat yourself to a wellness day at Ana Maria for a relaxing or deep muscle massage (30 to 90 minutes) or a body wrapping with aloe vera, etc.) and allow your soul to fly. Ana Maria is both competent and likeable and

Wellness in the caldera: bathe in the salt pans of Pedra de Lume

prices are reasonable. *Mon–Sat 10am–7pm | Santa Maria | the yellow house behind the Cazu supermarket | tel. 9 77 36 26 | FB*

FISH SPA

This tickles, at least in the beginning … Hundreds of small doctor fish (don't worry, they don't have any teeth!) nibble away at your feet, which dangle in the perspex basin. They give you a jolly pedicure which will make your feet as soft as a baby. While these tiny creatures do their work, you can enjoy a cold drink. *Mon–Sat | Santa Maria | tel. 9 19 86 16 | FB*

SALINAS

Allow yourself to get carried away – what's nice is that you can't sink. In the *salinas* of Pedra de Lume you paddle on the surface just like the Dead Sea, and your skin benefits from the high salt content. In addition, you can opt for a salt or mud massage or a facial. Afterwards, in the café, ask for the key to the shower (you will need it). *Daily 7am–6pm | admission 5 euros | FB*

FESTIVALS

A music festival on the white sandy beach of Santa Maria is a dream! These days almost 20,000 visitors turn up on 15 September for the annual pilgrimage to the *Festival Internacional de Santa Maria* (admission 5 euros). Over two days you can experience the stars of the Cape Verdean music scene as well as internationally renowned artists on the festival ground by the blue Atlantic Ocean. And as for the atmosphere … there's nothing like it. *festivalsantamaria.com*

NIGHTLIFE

Those who want hustle and bustle in the evening will find what they are looking for in *Santa Maria*. There are many pubs, bars and nightclubs, and Cape Verde's first ever casino. If you are looking for a drink in the afternoon, you will find a restaurant with a 🐖 happy hour *(daily 6.30–7.30pm)* on every other corner. The *Bar Tortue* on the top terrace of the Morabeza Hotel is the perfect place, with drinks at reduced prices.

INSIDER TIP
Half-price happiness

BUDDY

Locals and tourists have a good time together – the daily live music does the trick. *Daily. | Santa Maria | Rua 1 de Junho*

CALEMA PUB

The feel-good bar: their cool cocktails draw in the young surfer crowd. Almost always live music or a hip DJ sound. *Daily | Santa Maria | Rua 1 de Junho | FB*

CASINO ROYAL

The minimum stake for roulette is 1 euro, blackjack 2 euros and poker 3 euros. In addition, 75 slot machines either take your cash or multiply it, depending on your luck. However, the drinks are cheap (so that you'll be more likely to take a risk!). Make sure you bring your passport. *Daily 4pm–4am | Santa Maria | Av. dos Hoteis | casinoroyal.cv*

OCEAN CAFÉ

Superb selection of beers and cocktails, as much pizza as you can eat, live

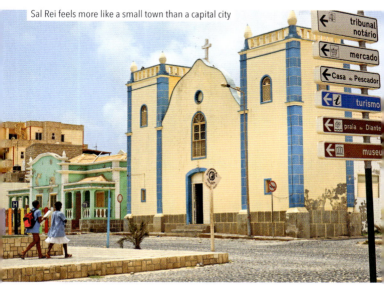

Sal Rei feels more like a small town than a capital city

==snorkelling on her small yacht *Spöki*: guaranteed fun!== If you are lucky, you will spot humpback whales between March and May and turtles laying their eggs on the beach from July to October. There's a money-back guarantee if none of the big animals turn up during the tour!

The international  *Turtle Foundation (Sal Rei | tel. 2 51 19 65 and 5 81 48 34 | turtle-foundation.org)* runs a turtle survey station on the island and invites interested visitors to join their beach patrols.

WATER SPORTS

The *Praia de Estoril* is the in place for all kinds of water sports and for all levels of expertise. There are numerous surfing and diving bases, such as

Paradise Kite School (paradisekite school.com), Boa Vista Wind Club (boavistawindclub.com) and *Kite Zone (kitezone-bubista.com)*, offering equipment and courses, the latter also rents out SUP boards. Experienced surfers and pros will find great conditions in the south, north and especially in the east: *Praia de Cabral (⬚ R9), Praia da Antónia (⬚ R–S8)* and *Praia das Gatas (⬚ S9)*. Beginners should stay in the *bay at Sal Rei* as it is protected by a barrier island just off the coast.

BEACHES

Boa Vista has the longest and most beautiful beaches of the Cape Verde Islands. The fine white Sahara sand

Statuettes à la Cape Verde made at the pottery school in Rabin

and the crystal-clear turquoise water are incomparable; the constant north-east trade wind is perfect for surfers. A bottle of water, sunscreen and a hat are all essential, and parasols and loungers are only available on the more frequented beaches!

PRAIA DA CHAVE

A beach that stretches for miles backed by high sand dunes. However, the idyllic beach is not an insider tip anymore: the local hotels host several thousands of holiday guests. *R9*

PRAIA DA VARANDINHA ★

The desert stretches down to the sea and the bizarre rock formations form an impressive backdrop for this beach. A grotto provides shade. It is extremely windy, but great for walks. There is a lighthouse on the limestone plateau at the westernmost point on Boa Vista, the *Ponta Varandinha*, but this beach is only accessible by 4x4. *R9*

PRAIA DE ESTORIL

The Praia de Estoril stretches around 10km south from Sal Rei. It is perfect for water sports which makes it very popular with young holidaymakers, but there are also families. In addition to the surfing and diving bases, there are beach umbrellas, sun loungers, restaurants and cafés. The Ilha de Sal Rei off the coast protects the bay from wind and waves. *R9*

PRAIA DE SANTA MÓNICA

This powdery white sandy beach stretches for an impressive 18km. It can only be reached in an off-road vehicle – preferably with a local driver or rented from one of the many organisations that offer this excursion for individuals or groups. *R10*

PRAIA DO CURRALINHO

The continuation of Praia de Santa Mónica, it is often too windy for swimming here but ideal for a walk along the beach. *R10*

WELLNESS

The five-star *Iberostar Hotel* allows non-residents to use their luxurious wellness area *(booking required at least 30 mins in advance | 10 euros/2 hrs | Praia da Chave | tel. 2 51 21 70 | iberostar.com).* Their bathing paradise includes a sauna, Turkish bath, whirlpool, gym, etc., while a massage comes at an additional charge.

INSIDER TIP
Relax!

FESTIVALS

On 4 July each year a big procession takes place in honour of *Santa Isabel*, the island's patron saint. The saint's statue, accompanied by church dignitaries in magnificent robes and a few hundred participants, is carried from the Catholic church in Sal Rei to Santa Barbara and back. The festival also features activities such as horse racing, a regatta, a football tournament and swimming competitions. There is a night of concerts (until the early morning!) and other wordly amusements. The town centre is host to numerous small stalls where people come to eat grilled food in the evening and drink beer or a liqueur or two.

NIGHTLIFE

BOA VISTA SOCIAL CLUB

Sit on the beach with a drink in hand and count the stars ... or just chat at the bar, listen to music and watch the world go by ... or make new friends. You can dance in the disco on Friday night. *Daily | Praia de Estoril | FB: boavistasocialclubcaboverde*

ESPLANADA MUNICIPAL SILVES

The *bobistas* (residents of Boa Vista) love the shady terrace around this kiosk for a number of reasons: the location is central, they serve tasty sandwiches and other snacks as well as a reasonably priced dish of the day and most of all there's cool live music on Friday night. *Daily | Sal Rei*

INSIDER TIP
Celebrate!

MORABEZA

This beach bar is by far the most popular! A cool ambience, interesting people, superb cocktails and always something new going on: reggae night, sunset party, drumming shows, fire eaters. During the day, the beach is great for relaxing. *Daily | Praia de Estoril | FB: morabeza.boavista*

Praia da Varandinha is a peaceful place, ideal for a leisurely beach walk

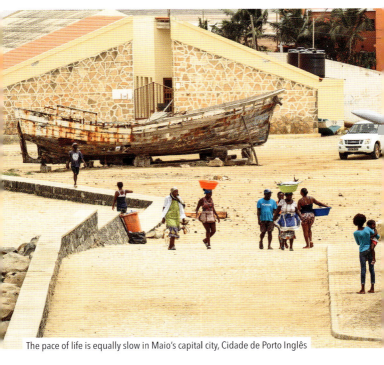

The pace of life is equally slow in Maio's capital city, Cidade de Porto Inglês

MAIO

(□ P–Q 14–16) **Silence reigns supreme on secluded Maio where nature has remained pristine.**

The smallest of the desert islands provides a refuge for both endangered animals such as the osprey and sea turtle as well as for stressed holidaymakers.

Rest and relaxation are the treasures that Maio has to offer. The fact that little Maio was not able to keep up with its sister islands in terms of development and progress has become a great advantage.

While Sal's and Boa Vista's main objective seems to be earning as much from tourism as possible, Maio does things differently. Time and silence are two of the few valuable things the island has no shortage of. The material wealth Maio once possessed – salt – was siphoned off by Portuguese and English traders in the 18th and 19th centuries. The island saw some of this prosperity in the form of a few colonial houses, a Catholic church and a fortress. But, at the same time, the feudal system was strengthened: decades after the abolishment of slavery on the other islands, hundreds of slaves were still at their

Despite this, most of the island (269km²) is made up of sparsely covered steppe and parched salt marshes. A few undulating hills of weathered volcanic craters and limestone rocks rise up in the middle and south-east of the island; the highest point is *Monte Penoso* (436m).

SIGHTSEEING

🔟 CIDADE DE PORTO INGLÊS ⭐

In 2014, the island's capital (pop. 3,000), Vila do Maio, recovered (almost) its original name, Cidade de Porto Inglês. In the 18th century it had been called Porto Inglês (English Port), after the English traders who used it to load salt from the salt works. The town lies on a high plateau. In the centre, the white church of *Nossa Senhora da Luz* stands at the top of some wide steps. On the church square there's a hotel, as well as a few cafés and shops. A little further on is the *Casa Cardoso*, a colonial house built for the island's richest salt trader at the beginning of the 20th century.

white masters' mercy on Maio, which was full of poverty and despair. Many of the inhabitants perished in the frequent droughts and famines; others escaped by emigrating.

Today, around 7,000 people live on Maio, most of them in the island's capital, Porto Inglês, on the southwest coast. The remainder have their homes in small villages near the road which circles the island. In contrast to the other two desert islands, there are many trees on Maio and there are even extensive acacia forests thanks to the reforestation activities in the north and west. There are also groves of palm trees in the coastal areas.

Above and below the church, little pastel-coloured painted houses enliven paved streets laid out in a grid pattern. Down by the sea is the cobbled *Avenida Amílcar Cabral* with its restaurants and *mini mercados*, banks and a health centre. A few people sit idly on a wall overlooking the broad sandy beach, colourful fishing boats lie in the light sand, and fishermen mend their nets nearby. At the southern end of the town, the little *Fortaleza (admission free)*, dating from the 18th century, still has its canons in place, and its blue painted wall tiles relate the history of the town. ▥ *P16*

🔢 SALT WORKS

The salt works start in Vila do Maio and continue north for around 5km. Plants that have adapted to the salty environment flourish in the glittering rosy pink and white hills of salt. They provide local and migratory birds with a suitable place to rest and feed. Free-roaming cattle pass the signposted nature reserve trail, and you can buy the harvested sea salt in the small salt works. ▥ *P15–16*

🔢 MORRO

The little village of Morro (pop. 300) is located on both sides of the ring road, in the midst of coconut palms. It is only a short walk to a magnificent beach. The *Ribeira do Morro* valley is especially interesting for amateur archaeologists: this is the spot where the oldest rocks in the archipelago were found. You can see the *Monte Batalha* (294m) in the north-east. *Around 5km north of Vila do Maio* | ▥ *P15*

🔢 ACACIA FORESTS 🎧

Reforestation projects have created two acacia forest that now cover an area of 3,500 hectares. They stretch from the road between Morro and Calheta to the east and between Cascabulho and Pedro Vaz to the north. Here you find many unique plant species and insects and plenty of grey-spotted guinea fowls that are typical on the island. It is also interesting to meet one of the many charcoal burners who live in tiny hamlets and

produce charcoal using traditional methods. ▥ *P–Q15*

🔢 CALHETA

Calheta is the second largest town (pop. 1,200) on the island. The small *church* on the main square has a sweeping white and yellow façade; visitors enter through the side chapel. There are one-storeyed houses in pastel shades on the main street, *Rua São José*, and in the straight, partly unpaved side streets. *Around 3km from Morro; 8km north of Porto Inglês* | ▥ *P15*

🔢 RIBEIRA DOM JOÃO

The Ribeira Dom João valley stretches in a green oasis from the plateau all the way down to the sea. A grove of palm trees on the outskirts of the village of the same name (pop. 200) stretches almost to the mouth of the river that flows to a wonderful beach with fine, white sand. *Around 12km east of Porto Inglês (turn off in Figueira Seca)* ▥ *Q15–16*

EATING & DRINKING

BIG GAME MAIO

The environment of quad bikes and big-game fishing may deter some, but the Italian cuisine is marvellous with lots of fish, seafood and Italian wines. Good value for money. *Daily* | *Porto Inglês* | *Av. Amílcar Cabral* | *tel. 9 71 05 93* | *FB* | *€*

CENTRUM SETE SÓIS, SETE LUAS

The cultural centre Seven Suns, Seven Moons is on a mission to promote and celebrate Cape Verdean culture. The centre has seven branches (on Santo Antão, Santiago, Fogo, Brava and Maio) and is a project instigated by the music festival of the same name that has been celebrated on these islands every autumn for 20 years.

INSIDER TIP
Win-win fun

==Music, art and gastronomy are used here to create opportunities for young people in Cape Verde as well as to showcase the versatility of the country to its visitors.== Pay them a visit! They have an extensive menu with lots of fresh ingredients when available. Vegetarians will love their colourful and varied creations. *Closed Mon | Porto Inglês | Av. Amílcar Cabral | tel. 9 95 06 01 | €*

NEPTUNO

A tiny space and a few tables on the pavement, but the grilled fish is fabulous, as is the pizza. If you want to risk eating an ice cream, you may find a sweet heaven. *Daily | Porto Inglês | Av. Amílcar Cabral | tel. 9 93 37 56 | €*

SHOPPING

LOJA DE ARTESANATO

Here, the artisans from Maio present their handicrafts made out of materials from the ocean: shells, driftwood, buoys, fishing nets, etc., plus pottery and stonecraft, metal figurines, jewellery and more. *Porto Inglês | opposite Fortaleza*

As usual, local people can give you the best restaurant recommendations

SPORT & ACTIVITIES

EXCURSIONS

People with plenty of energy can walk for miles along the white sandy beaches and enjoy the views. There are many worthwhile destinations in the interior of the island and the *Monte Batalha* (294m) and *Monte Penoso* (436m) offer some height. Bernard and Valérie from *A Caminhada (tel. 5 95 69 69 | maio-cap-vert.net)* in Morro will be pleased to offer advice and guided tours for hikers.

The *Fundação Maio Biodiversidade (Porto Inglês | tel. 3 55 62 42 | fmb-maio.org)*, a nature conservation foundation, is dedicated to the preservation of the nature on Maio and the creation of a sustainable livelihood. It offers information and a series of great excursions ranging from turtle- and birdwatching to the history of salt production.

SNORKELLING & DIVING

The *Dive Centre (Porto Inglês | tel. 9 51 81 02 | capvert-plongee.com)* run by Bernard and Catherine will take you snorkelling and diving in the beautiful turquoise ocean. They can't be missed between the two beach bars on the main beach. You just have to see the amazing underwater world, and especially for beginners who will embark on an incredible adventure.

BEACHES

There are beautiful beaches all around the island. The beaches on the west coast are ideal for swimming – a beach of fine sand stretches for miles from Porto Inglês to past Calheta. The treacherous currents make the beaches in the north of the island unsuitable for swimming. This is where the sea turtles lay their eggs in summer and you should stay away from the beach during this time. There are also heavenly beaches in the east and south but they are more difficult to reach. You have to take drinking water, food and protection you from the sun!

PONTA PRETA

A high plateau south of Vila do Maio that has unfortunately been defaced by uncontrolled development. The perfect, golden sandy beach with small caves in the colourful rocks stretches for 6km to the east. Due to the strong currents it is not always suitable for swimming, but hikers can admire the beautiful images which the surf creates on the sand. *P16*

PRAIA DE MORRO

Magnificent white sandy beach, and while its dangerous currents make it unsuitable for swimming, it is perfect for a walk. However, a large holiday complex in the dunes disturbs the idyll somewhat. *P15*

PRAIA DE PAU SECO

This rocky beach on the west coast is well suited for snorkelling. It can be

reached by walking along the beach from Calheta. *P15*

PRAIA DE SANTANA ⭐

A somewhat hidden beach – with 25m high dunes – north-west of Morrinho. Although there are strong winds, it is suitable for swimming. Walkers can find bizarre boulders and desert roses here.

PRAIA DO PORTO INGLÊS

On the fine, white sand of the island's capital, two beach bars provide shade and cold drinks while colourful fishing boats make it picture-perfect. *P16*

NIGHTLIFE

BAR TIBAU

Tibau Tavares is one of Cape Verde's best-known musicians. When he's not on tour, he can be found working at his own little *mercearia* and a café: two tables and chairs on the pavement. You'll always see locals here chatting about music and everyday matters over their favourite tipple. *Porto Inglês | Av. Amílcar Cabral, opposite Tutti Frutti | FB: tibau.tavares.cv*

INSIDER TIP
Talk music with a VIP

TROPIKAL

This colourful beach bar is *the* Maio hotspot for holidaymakers, both during the day and especially in the evening. Open until late at night. The loungers and chairs in the sand are for tourists and local people alike. They serve chips, omelettes, pizza made from fresh ingredients or *catch-upa*, the national Cape Verdean dish. If you haven't tried it, do so after the happy hour *(5–7pm)* when caipirinha is the favourite. *Tue–Sun, Sat from 10pm live music | Porto Inglês | FB: tropikalmaio*

Turtles lay their eggs in the fine sand on the beaches on Maio's north coast

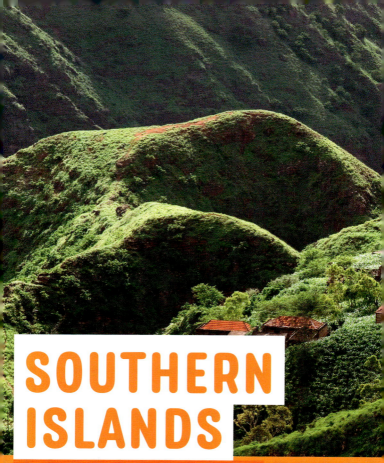

SOUTHERN ISLANDS

Traces left by the Portuguese colonial rulers can be found everywhere on the southern islands as this is where the Portuguese first embarked on the risky business of settling in the tropics.

On the previously uninhabited islands, the Portuguese constructed fortresses, churches and convents, and, later on, magnificent country houses and townhouses, the so-called *sobrados*. You can find these in picturesque São Filipe on Fogo or mist-shrouded Nova Sintra on Brava.

A hiker's paradise on Santiago: the Serra Malagueta

Cidade Velha on Santiago, the old capital and former centre of the slave trade, is a historical hotspot and UNESCO World Heritage Site. Today, colourful fishing boats land their catch in the spot where, in 1585, privateer Sir Francis Drake loaded his booty onto ships destined for England. Columbus, Darwin and Vasco da Gama also visited the islands.

The southern islands are perfect for hiking, and the Pico do Fogo volcano is not just the highest peak but also the focal point.

SOUTHERN ISLANDS

OCEANO
ATLÂNTICO

Praia do Tarrafal

6 Tarrafal ★

Pedra Ferro

Achada Monte

Ribeira da Prata

Ponta Verde

Calheta de São Miguel

5 Serra Malagueta

Cancelo

Pedra Badejo

Porto de Ribeira da Barca

Achada Fazenda

Assomada **4**

Santiago
p.70

Pícos

João Teves

Porto Rincão

72km, 2½ hrs

Rui Vaz **3**

São Domingos

Achadinha

Ribeirão Chiqueiro

Porto Mosquito

São João Ba(p)tista

Salineiro

6km, 10 mins

Praia ★ **1**

Cidade Velha ★ **2**

Prainha

8 km
4.97 mi

SANTIAGO

(Ⓜ M–O 14–17) **Santiago is the main island of Cape Verde and, at 991km², it is also the largest. Nowhere else in Cape Verde are there more houses, more cars, more doctors, more money or more crime. Santiago is the island of superlatives.**

The topography is formed by two mighty mountain ranges: the *Pico d'Antónia* nature reserve with the highest mountain on the island (1,394m) and the Serra Malagueta (1,064m). In between, there is a series of intensively cultivated, high, steep-sided plateaus. More than half of all Cape Verdeans live here – around 290,000 – and two of the three largest cities in Cape Verde are on Santiago. These are the capital city Praia and the dynamic centre of agricultural trade Assomada.

Santiago is the most African of all the islands. Its culture and traditions are characterised by an especially strong African influence because this island always had the closest ties to the continent. This is particularly noticeable in the music and language. The islanders call themselves *badios* in contrast to the *sampadjudos* – their name for the inhabitants of the other islands.

WHERE TO START?

Up to the plateau! That is the centre of Praia and it is where you'll find all of the capital's interesting sights: the old colonial houses, town hall and church, the culture centre, the vegetable market and Museu Etnográfico are only a few minutes' walk away from each other. The journey here from the airport takes only ten minutes by taxi.

SIGHTSEEING

1 PRAIA ⭐

Cape Verde's capital city is located in the south-east of Santiago. The city (pop. 145,000) succeeded Cidade Velha (15km away) as the seat of government in 1770 because it had one decisive advantage: a 40m-high plateau that was easy to defend against pirates. From that time on, things improved for the city and its population steadily grew. Praia has now come to set the tone in lifestyle, art and culture.

The *plateau* still forms the centre of the city. Women carrying heavy bowls of fruit on their head, money changers and shoe polishers offer their services – it is a busy place but you'll come across Cape Verdean laissez faire as well. The renovated two-storey ▌*vegetable market* sells pretty much anything that grows on the islands. It is noisy and crowded and all the different smells blend into each other: welcome to Africa! One of the colourful houses on the main square *Praça de Albuquerque* has been turned into the 🐖 *Palácio da Cultura Ildo Lobo (Mon–Fri 9am–noon, 2.30–6.30pm, Sat 10am–1pm | admission free | Av.*

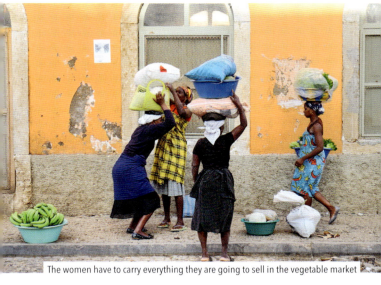

The women have to carry everything they are going to sell in the vegetable market

Amílcar Cabral 17 | FB | ⏱ 45 mins). This cultural centre doesn't always have an extensive schedule of events, but at least there will be an exhibition to explore. Don't miss their musical events in the evening! Close by are the town hall and the Catholic church *Nossa Senhora da Graça.* If you are interested in how people here used to live in the past, the *Museu Etnográfico de Cabo Verde (Tue–Fri 9am–5pm, Sat 9am–2pm | admission 200 CVE | Rua 5 de Julho 45 | FB | ⏱ 30 mins)* displays its treasures in the pedestrian precinct. Historical articles and exhibits of everyday life describe the way life used to be on the different islands.

Shopping Cape Verdean style: below the plateau is the 🌡🚩 *sucupira* market that sells all kinds of goods *(Mon–Sat).* You will find mountains of shoes next to the latest electronic toys

from China; right alongside, bikinis in all the colours of the rainbow flutter in the breeze; at the next stand T-shirts, football jerseys and fabrics with colourful African patterns flap in the wind next to sparkling ball gowns … If you are looking for a new style, 💇 nimble fingers will transform your hair into little braids.

The upper-class *Prainha* district is on a peninsula to the west. Stately diplomats' villas and private estates surround well-manicured parks and form the perfect backdrop for elegant hotels with panoramic views of the Prainha and Quebra Canela beaches. There is even a modern shopping centre with a cinema and also an upmarket casino that is currently being constructed.

The shrine of Cape Verdean football fans is 8km outside Praia: the *National*

Colourful fishing boats on the beach of Tarrafal await their next trip

Stadium accommodates 15,000 spectators and it is here where the national team Tubarões Azuis (blue sharks) is enthusiastically supported. Its biggest success until now was to participate in the African Cup of Nations in 2013 *N17*

2 CIDADE VELHA ★

This is where settlement of the archipelago began. Immediately after their discovery, the Portuguese claimed the Cape Verde Islands as a colony and the first military base started operating within months. Four years later, the first settlers arrived. Due to its favourable location between Africa, Europe and America, Ribeira Grande became a major hub of the slave trade and made the Portuguese crown immensely wealthy. However, these riches attracted pirates like Francis

Drake and Jacques Cassart; famous Portuguese navigators like Vasco da Gama also stopped over here. You are walking on historic ground (see Discovery Tour 1 on p. 121)! The colonial buildings in Cidade Velha (pop. 1,200) were declared UNESCO World Heritage Sites in 2009. *N17*

3 RUI VAZ

The village of Rui Vaz (pop. 1,000) lies at an altitude of 800m in the midst of breathtaking mountain scenery. This is the starting point for visits to the *Pico d'Antónia* nature reserve with Monte Xoxa and all its antennas. A narrow, steep path leads down (400m) from the village to *São Jorge dos Orgãos* where Cape Verde's agricultural research institute has been established. They also run a small botanical garden (Jardim Botánico |

no set opening times | admission 200 CVE). *N16*

4 ASSOMADA

If you're planning on visiting Assomada (pop. 15,000), then you must go on a Wednesday or Saturday – ⚑ market days. The market is the engine and heart of the city, a folksy, popular venue with a brisk trade in everything from pigs and chickens to clothes, baskets, fish and bananas. The Catholic church and town hall are on the main square, the *Praça Gustavo Monteiro,* where you can also find a bust of national hero Amílcar Cabral. *M16*

5 SERRA MALAGUETA

The Serra Malagueta is in the north of the island. Until well into the 1980s, when a road was built through the rugged range, the more than 1,000m-high mountains separated Tarrafal from the rest of Santiago. The Serra Malagueta is now a nature reserve and a real highlight for hiking. It has 26 species of endemic plants as well as the Cape Verde kingfisher, national symbol of the islands.

A small ⚑ *shop (Mon–Fri 9am–4pm | on the road from Assomada to Tarrafal)* in the park administration building sells *panos* and other authentic Cape Verdean arts and crafts. Brochures in English and Portuguese provide information on the nature reserve; there is also a toilet and small snack bar. Approaching from Praia, the entrance to the national park is 100m before the shop. If the cabin is

manned, you pay 200 CVE admission; if not, you are in luck. *M15*

6 TARRAFAL ⭐

Tarrafal (pop. 8,000) is located in the hot north-west of Santiago. The small semi-circular bay has a beach of white sand fringed with coconut palms. A dozen colourful fishing boats lie on the edge of the ocean. The fishermen set out in their boats shortly before sunrise and return around midday when the market women gather at the shore to inspect the day's catch. As soon as the shopkeepers have carried away their selection in large bowls, peace returns to the coast.

The name Tarrafal brings back painful memories in Portugal as the former concentration camp – where the facist Salazar regime used to torture and murder resistance fighters and critics – is just a few miles away. A tiny *museum (daily 8am–6pm | admission 100 CVE)* displays pictures and documents (only in Portuguese). *M15*

EATING & DRINKING

BATUKU

Is it Cape Verdean cuisine with a Brazilian touch or the other way round? Just try it ...

INSIDER TIP
Brazil meets Cape Verde

Here you can enjoy true culinary delights, sitting in a cosy courtyard where passion fruits hang from the ceiling, refreshed by a gentle Atlantic breeze. They sometimes have live music *(batuku). Closed Mon | Cidade Velha | Rua Banana | tel. 9 76 18 69 | FB | €€–€€€*

CAFÉ PÃO QUENTE

Just follow your nose: it will lead you straight to a huge selection of tasty bread and cake specialities from their own bakery. To take away or eat in at one of several branches. *Daily | Praia | Plateau | Rua Andrade Corvo 16 | €*

CASA STRELA

The B&B managed by Andreas is a little corner of paradise. Breakfast à la carte, a sundowner or local specialties for dinner? Delightfully furnished, a wonderful roof terrace with sea view, great service, excursions and advice on offer – you're in good hands here. *Daily | Tarrafal | Whatsapp 9 17 85 29 | strela-adventure-tarrafal.com | €€*

LINHA D'AGUA

Eat and chill listening to the waves: directly by the small hidden Prainha Beach opposite the Oasis Atlântico Praiamar Hotel. The daily menu comprises one fish and one meat dish. *Daily | Praia | tel. 2 62 36 76 | FB | €€*

NHAMII ICE DREAMS

Exotic, delicious home-made ice cream using wonderful tropical fruit such as mango, passion fruit, coconut and guava. Why not try *bissap* (hibiscus flower), *komoka* (roasted sweetcorn) and *calabaceira* (baobab)? *Daily | Praia | Platô | Rua 5 de Julho | FB*

INSIDER TIP
Changing varieties

PIZZERIA ALTO MIRA

The *peixe do dia* is always fresh and as delicious as the stone-baked pizza. Other fish dishes are also very good. Friendly vibe in a charming courtyard. *Closed Sun & lunchtime | Tarrafal | tel. 9 96 38 65 & 9 28 29 83 | FB | €*

Always fresh and tasty: *bife de atum* (tuna steak)

SANTIAGO FISHING

Look out to sea, enjoy a cold drink and listen to the music … You may want to chat with other guests or just read a good book … And the food is delicious, with the freshly caught fish being served within minutes. *Daily | Cidade Velha | Rua Cadjau | tel. 9 14 77 34 | €€*

SHOPPING

The markets on Santiago are particularly colourful and lively. In *Praia* the vegetable market (see p. 70) and the *sucupira* (see p. 71), where all kinds of goods are sold, are open from Monday to Saturday; it is also worth visiting *Assomada* on Wednesday or Saturday.

PONTO CV

Your return flight is a little while off, you have some escudos left in your pocket and are still looking for souvenirs for family and friends? **Here is your chance to browse a complete selection** from the islands' foods: coffee, Fogo wine, *grogue*, tuna from São Nicolau! Or try another Cape Verdean dish before you board the plane: they serve the national dish *cachupa* in many varieties, even with black pudding! *Daily | Praia | Achada St Antonio, opposite the Hotel Roterdão | FB*

SPORT & ACTIVITIES

DIVECENTER SANTIAGO

Having returned from your dive, enjoy the sunset over Fogo with a cold drink and marvel at your fabulous adventure under the sea. Diving instructor Georg and his colleague Monaya are known experts in the local diving community, especially in underwater archaeology. *Tarrafal | Ponta d'Atum | tel. 9 93 64 07 | FB*

STRELA ADVENTURE TARRAFAL

Strela Adventure come up with great suggestions for adventures in and around Tarrafal! Whether it's an island tour, hiking or mountain biking, surfing or snorkelling – you certainly won't get bored. Try their "fish 'n' grill" offer, where you catch your own fish for grilling, **or go kayaking on the Atlantic Ocean!**

INSIDER TIP
A surfing alternative

Tarrafal | WhatsApp 9 17 85 29 | tours.strela-travel.com/

TUTUTOURS

Being out and about with Tutu means that you get to know Cape Verde well and will be greatly entertained. With a wonderful American accent, the Brava-born "Champion of Guides" explains what makes Santiago tick. Hikes, city walks and island tours by car. *Praia | tel. 9 84 67 91 | tututours2@gmail.com*

BEACHES

PRAIA DO TARRAFAL

The island's showpiece beach is located in a sheltered bay in the northwest. It has dreamy soft white sand, is lined with palm trees and part of a genuine fishing village. Wonderful for swimming, relaxing or just watching. *M15*

PRAINHA/QUEBRA CANELA

Praia's two bathing beaches are located to the left and right of the *Ponta Temerosa* promontory and its lighthouse. With their white sand between dark rocks and a couple of acacia trees to provide some shade, they are especially popular with families and at weekends. Please note that the *Praia de Gamboa* below the *plateau* isn't clean enough for bathing. *N17*

FESTIVALS

FESTIVAL MANUEL GAMBOA

Praia's town celebration day, 19 May, with a marvellous music festival was until recently held on the Praia de Gamboa, but has been moved to make space for a newly constructed hotel complex. Three nights of entertainment until the early morning with well-known bands and musicians from Cape Verde, Brazil, the Caribbean and Africa.

KRIOL JAZZ FESTIVAL

INSIDER TIP
Cabo Verde jams

Cape Verdean jazz? Hello! Early to mid-April local stars and upcoming talent as well as jazz musicians from the rest of the world meet in Praia to jam and groove. *Praia | Praça Luis de Camões | krioljazzfestival.com*

NIGHTLIFE

The town beach *Quebra Canela* and its surroundings are a nightlife hotspot in Praia. The pubs directly above the ocean serve good food, play cool music and attract an interesting crowd. If you have got your beach towel with you, you can jump straight into the sea. The *Praia Shopping*, Cape Verde's first ever and only shopping mall, is only a few steps away. Here you find more chic restaurants and a cinema with several screens showing the l atest Hollywood blockbusters.

5AL DA MÚSICA

You simply must go! The restaurant is actually famous for the unforgettable performances given by famous musicians, but the chef is also an artist in his own right. Live music every evening; *batuco* dancers swing their hips on Tuesdays. *Mon–Sat | Praia | Plateau | Av. Amílcar Cabral 70*

KAZA BRANKA

A fun mixture of pub, restaurant and nightclub. The nightclub, in particular, attracts the young in-crowd from the entire region because of the venue's location in the hip Palmarejo quarter. The clientele guarantees a good, relaxed atmosphere, sometimes as early as lunchtime, but certainly at 3am. *Daily | Praia | Praça Palmarejo*

FOGO

(ᴗ G–H 16–18) **The name says it all: the island of Fogo (Portuguese for fire) is an active volcano. Circular, almost 3,000m high, it has a cone measuring 25km at the base and** 9km at the top of the caldera, *Chã das Caldeiras*.

The base of the crater is at an altitude of around 1,700m and is enclosed to the west by a gigantic semicircle of jagged, almost 1,000m-high walls of rock. The perfectly shaped cone – the Pico do Fogo – rises out of the bizarre black and grey lava ash landscape on the eastern edge. It is 2,829m high, making it the highest mountain in Cape Verde. Enormous rivers of lava – pitch black or grey depending on their age – snake their way down from the caldera to the ocean and hot sulphurous vapours force their way out of gaping vents on the precipitous eastern flank.

The north-east side of the island benefits from the trade winds that

Palm trees rustle and bend in the wind on Praia do Tarrafal

make it fertile and very green. Citrus, mango, banana trees and coffee bushes give the area around Mosteiros on the coast a feeling of the tropics. This is also where you will find the forested Monte Velha area: a dense forest of eucalyptus trees and conifers. There are fertile volcanic ash fields on the northern slopes where the grapes that are used to produce the *vinho de Fogo* grow in shallow hollows.

There is even agriculture. Apart from grapes, the inhospitable looking lunar landscape is great for growing tomatoes, sweet potato, manioc and Congo beans as well as papaya, figs, apples, quince and even peaches. The total population of the 476-km² island is 37,000. Approximately half of them live in the São Filipe region on the west side and a quarter in the north, near Mosteiros. A ring road around the island, partly cobbled and partly tarmacked, connects the isolated farmsteads and villages.

SIGHTSEEING

7 SÃO FILIPE ⭐

The capital of the island (pop. 10,000) is located on a 70m-high plateau on the south-west coast. It was founded around 1500 as the second settlement on Cape Verde. Portuguese aristocratic families were granted the land from the crown and a strict hierarchy was established. The aristocratic class lived in the lower town *(Bila Baixo)* separated by a wall from the slaves who lived in the upper town *(Bila Riba)*. The segregation waned over time, as evidenced by the development of a mixed Creole society. The social differences were also reflected in the architecture of the houses, with the rich living in elegant *sobrados* – two-storey houses with balconies and airy central courtyards. The most beautiful of these are now listed buildings – one of them is a private museum run by Monique Widmer, a Swiss expat. The ☛ *Casa da Memória (Wed–Fri 10am–noon and by appointment | admission free, donations welcome | Rua do Mercado | tel. 2 81 27 65 | casadamemoria.com.cv | ⏱ 1–2 hrs)* has furniture, household objects and historical photos, as well as a garden with endemic plants.

The 🏛 *Museu Municipal de São Filipe (Mon–Fri 8am–4pm | admission 100 CVE | Rua do Mercado | ⏱ 1 hr)* is just a few houses away. Along with the other exhibits explaining the island's colonial history, you will be able to see a typical slave hut *(funco)* in the courtyard.

The *Igreja Nossa Senhora da Conceição* with its sky-blue façade and the town hall are both located in the lower town. The *vegetable market* is just around the corner. There is plenty of hustle and bustle in the neighbouring streets in the morning. Women sell their fruit and fish on the roadside while loud hammering and sawing can be heard coming from the many carpenters' workshops. North American jeeps and motorbikes bump along over the potholed road.

Around 1850, Fogo's inhabitants began working on North American whalers which were hunting off Cape Verde, thereby establishing close ties

Immerse yourself in the daily life of Cape Verde at the vegetable market in São Filipe

with the US. Today, the biggest community of Cape Verdean expats can be found around Boston, Massachusetts. Therefore, don't be surprised to hear people on Fogo and its small neighbouring island of Brava speaking with a broad US accent.

The Praia da Fonte Bila with its glittering black sand stretches for miles below the steep coastline. The former fortress *Fortim Carlota*, which served as a prison until 2005, dominates the landscape. A paved path leads down to the beach below the fortress. Unfortunately, it is no longer safe there – do not walk on the beach by yourself! You don't have to fear being attacked in the city itself, since there are always plenty of people nearby. *G17*

🞱 NOS CRIOLA BONITA

German expat Ralph has a dream: in the west of the island, at around 900m above sea level, he has been creating a botanical garden since 2012, gradually transforming former agricultural areas into a green oasis of endemic plants. From here you can hike to an impressive kapok tree (90 minutes one way) or a small hidden spring (60 minutes). Ralph's wife Ella will open up their small restaurant for you on request and preferably by appointment *(daily | €)*. *Aleixo Gomes | tel. 2 81 41 98 and 5 89 81 78 | G17*

INSIDER TIP
Hiking through greenery

A hike across the lava slopes of the Chã das Caldeiras is unforgettable

9 CHÃ DAS CALDEIRAS ★

This caldera (Portuguese: *caldeira*), the collapsed crater of this ancient volcano, has a diameter of 9km. Black fields of boulders, grey fields of ash and tall tongues of lava create a bizarre scenery. Until Pico Pequeno last erupted in November 2014, there were two villages *Bangaeira* and *Portela* and a few smaller hamlets here, with a population of around 1,000. The villages were completely engulfed by lava during the eight-week natural catastrophe. Now all you can see is just a few roofs of the houses. Luckily, no one was injured but the inhabitants of the caldera lost both their homes and their livelihoods – from agriculture and tourism.

The first people to return took less than a year to re-establish their newly built guesthouses and other businesses. Although the government had advised against their return, they were helped further with generous donations from home and abroad. However, a road connecting the rebuilt villages took until 2019 to be completed. The people up here are reliant on "their" volcano, both emotionally and economically.

Quite a few of the former inhabitants of Chã das Caldeiras share a common ancestor: Count Armand de Montrond. As a result, many children have blonde hair and blue eyes – in contrast to their brown skin. The French nobleman settled on Fogo in 1872, built irrigation channels and roads, improved the medical care and introduced winegrowing to the Caldeira. *H17*

10 PICO DO FOGO ★

The gigantic shield volcano Pico do Fogo, simply referred to as Pico or Pico Grande, hasn't spat any fire out of the main cone at its peak since 1680. A hike on the 500m-wide and 150m-deep craters takes around four or five hours and you will be rewarded with magnificent views into the caldera and often across the Atlantic as far as Santiago. Hikers will have to deal with a 1,100-m difference in altitude so will need to be in good physical shape, have a head for heights and a sturdy pair of hiking shoes. It is compulsory to be accompanied by a guide, and you can get recommendations on certified guides at your accommodation. It is best to start as early as possible, maybe even at night under the magnificent sky, which up here is free from light pollution.

However, the way down will be the most memorable when, within a few minutes, you descend 500m, almost running down the steep ash slopes. Then, covered in dust and with a smile on your face, you sit at the bottom of the mountain and marvel at your accomplishment while emptying the ash out of your boots. *H17*

11 PICO PEQUENO/PICO 2014

The crater that erupted in 1995 and that spat lava again in November 2014 is on the western flank of the Pico. You have to climb up a good 400m through sharp-edged black lava before you can look into the caldera. Yellow sulphur and red iron oxide deposits paint bizarre images on the

black basalt, there is the smell of sulphur in the air and if you put some dry grass into one of the cracks in the rocks it will suddenly burst into flame. The spectacular backdrop is formed by two gigantic gas craters. We recommend that you take a guide for your hike through the newly created lava field because the crevices, loose rubble and falling rocks can be hazardous. *H17*

12 MONTE VELHA 🌡️

In the 1940s, acacia, cypress, pine and eucalyptus trees were planted on a large scale on the northern flank of the Pico do Fogo. Today the forest on Monte Velha is one of the largest wooded areas on Cape Verde. It is always cool and misty here; the delicate yellow and green lichens that cover the trees collect water from the air and transform the forest into a surreal wonderland ideal for walking. *H16*

13 MOSTEIROS

Mosteiros (pop. 1,200) lies in the green, subtropical north-east of the island in a picturesque location between steep mountain slopes and the ocean. In the centre time seems to stand still and a few rather run-down colonial houses are remnants of the past. The *church square* is right on the waterfront and provides a lovely view of the rocky coast. Coffee, papaya, mango and banana plants flourish on the green slopes above the town. The main growing region for Fogo coffee is in the area around Mosteiros. Even Starbucks has now included it in their

"Reserve" product range. Today, more than 100 tonnes of this strong, organic Arabica coffee are harvested each year. *H16*

EATING & DRINKING

FRONTEIRA

True explorers will be rewarded with hearty authentic Cape Verdean cuisine *(cachupa)*, but first you need to find this restaurant which is hidden in the steep road above the Hotel Xaguate. *Daily | São Filipe | Rua Francisco d'Arcanja | tel. 2 81 25 34 | €–€€*

MÊ D'RUA

Since April 2019, Fogo has a new gourmet temple: Frenchman Olivier uses fresh local produce for his few but spectacular dishes. Plus there's live music. Don't miss it! *Daily | São Filipe | next to the Hotel Savana | tel. 2 81 20 09 | FB | €*

TCHON DI CAFÉ

An excursion makes you feel hungry! This café in Mosteiros offers a shady place to eat: in the courtyard under the large almond tree, good home-made food will restore your spirit.

A walk through São Filipe's lower town leads to the church and beach

Daily | opposite the petrol station | tel. 2 83 16 10 | €

TORTUGA

Roberto from Italy has made his dream a reality and runs a small B&B on the black beach of São Filipe. Over lunch, between noon and 2pm, you can discuss with him what you would like to eat, but in the evening (booking required!) he is solely in charge! Roberto chose the location strategically because it is where the fishermen of São Filipe land their catch, which means that he has first choice. Here, you can get the whole thing for the cost of a seafood starter in Europe. *Daily | São Filipe | Praia Nossa Senhora de Encarnação | tel. 9 94 15 12 | €-€€*

INSIDER TIP
Prime position

TROPICAL

Colourful murals and subtropical decor under shady trees. Traditional and international cuisine, fish specialities. Try the "Romeo and Juliet" dessert. Cocktails in the evening, live music on Fridays from 11pm. *Daily | São Filipe | tel. 2 81 21 61 | €-€€*

SHOPPING

COOPERATIVA DO VINHO CHÃ

The Chã's wine cooperative has a new base at the foot of the caldera wall where it sells unique local specialities: wonderful red and white wine, fruity pomace liqueurs *(bagaceira)*, pomegranate liqueur and more. *Chã das Caldeiras*

DJA'R FOGO

The Agnelo family has been planting and roasting coffee for six generations. Today, it is packaged and sold in pretty cotton bags. They also offer other souvenirs made of banana leaves or recycled materials. A shady patio invites visitors for a coffee break. *São Filipe | Rua D Costa (a crossroads close to the church)*

INSIDER TIP
A kick for coffee lovers

PADARIA MARIA AUGUSTA

The baker takes the most delicious biscuits, which Dona Maria Augusta has prepared according to her traditional recipe, out of the huge oven using a long-handled shovel. You get a whole bag for 100 CVE! The place isn't that easy to find: it is the orange house on the square near the Catholic church, opposite the former prison *(fortim)*. Enter from the sea-facing side and climb a couple of steps on the right to the anteroom of the bakery. *Closed Sun | São Filipe*

SPORT & ACTIVITIES

CLIMBING

Climbing and bouldering in the region: *Mustafa Eren (Chã das Caldeiras | tel. 9 79 23 22 | musti@ revolutionclimbing.eu)* is a mountain guide as well as being a trainer for sport climbing who will guide you up or down in the volcano area. The gigantic crater wall around the caldera is the perfect place for one- or two-day climbing treks and you will also be taken into the depths of two eruption caves. High-quality equipment provided.

HIKING IN THE BORDEIRA

Have you ever heard the ocean waves from an altitude of 2,500m? The Bordeira on Fogo is the remnant of the caldera of the original volcano, and its highest point (Atalaia, 2,760m) is almost at the level of the Pico do Fogo (which can get quite crowded). You will hike some 30km over two days through the rugged landscape with your (booked via your accommodation). Please note that a head for heights is essential. You will

sleep in a tent or under the stars in an incomparable sky. In the morning you wake up to a magnificent view of the Pico do Fogo volcano on one side and the Atlantic ocean with the neighbouring island of Brava on the other.

BEACHES

The strong surf and treacherous currents make bathing dangerous on Fogo. Even if you to see locals swimming you shouldn't follow them.

PONTA DA SALINA

The island's best swimming beach is around 15km north-west of São Filipe. A rocky bridge separates a pool from the ocean. There is a small sandy beach between grottoes, caves and black basalt reefs. You can get cold drinks and there is also a loo. It's accessible from the road to São Jorge where a narrow road branches off down to the coast. *G–H16*

PRAIA DA FONTE BILA

The wide, black sandy beach below São Filipe stretches for miles – but swimming is dangerous. *G17*

FESTIVALS

FESTA DE NHÔ FILIPE

Fogo's biggest festival by far brings the island to a standstill for several weeks when the island's emigrants return for a home visit and proudly showcase their wealth, which they have mostly acquired in thew US. Hotels, ferries and flights are fully booked, and from around 20 April the concerts, tournaments and processions start.

The horse races attract competitors from as far afield as the northern islands. The highlight is on 1 May when the island's discovery is celebrated. Sand from the beach is carried onto the street above the market in São Filipe and horses and riders demonstrate their skills, encouraged by a cheering crowd.

NIGHTLIFE

BAR RAMIRO

Chã without Ramiro's bar? Ramiro would not let that happen! He and his son David re-opened this traditional bar up in the volcanic crater as soon as they could after the 2014 eruption. And the new place still sticks to the old, well-known recipe for success: original live music and self-pressed wine *(manecom)* lure plenty of people here! *Daily* | *Chã das Caldeiras* | *Portela*

BRAVA

(□□ F17–18) **Circular and hardly 10km in diameter: with an area of 64km², Brava (pop. 6,800) is the smallest of the inhabited islands of Cape Verde.**

The island is located in the south-west of the archipelago about 20km away from Fogo. The peaks of the almost 1,000m-high mountains are usually hidden under clouds because Brava lies in the lee of Fogo.

This is an advantage that has moulded the character of the island: the cloud cover means that the dew does not evaporate and benefits the island's vegetation which is luxuriant. From October to February Brava is an

Fogo wine gets its special aroma from the volcanic ash

oasis with verdant pastures, man-high maize and flowers blossoming everywhere. In this season, Brava's nickname of the "flower island" is completely justified: oleander, bougainvillea, jasmine and hibiscus in every shade imaginable blossom during these months. Dragon trees also becomes. The island capital *Nova Sintra* is at an altitude of 500m while the highest point, the mountain range *Monte Fontainhas* (976m), is 3km to the south. The sleepy village of *Fajã d'Água* lies on the west coast. Things were much livelier in the 19th century when North American

Even dragon trees grow on the island of Brava

grow here. However, the aridity of the past hundred years has made the springs and summers considerably more barren than in former times.

Visitors arrive at the island via the port of *Furna* on the east coast: a handful of cube-shaped houses makes its way up the hill behind the tiny bay. A cobblestone street leads steeply upwards, while bushy acacia branches hang down over the lanes and prickly agaves cling to rocky ledges. The higher you go, the cooler the air

whaling ships signed on seamen and loaded provisions here. The close relationship of the islanders to the east coast of the United States continues to this day.

From a geological viewpoint, Brava is actually an extension of Fogo: volcanic activity there can be felt as quakes on Brava. Work on the island is scarce as its isolated location is a hindrance to economic progress. So far, there is hardly any infrastructure for tourism. Connections by sea to

Fogo and Santiago have become much more reliable with the introduction of the Cabo Verde Fast Ferry, but if you plan to visit Brava, you should be flexible and allow a day or two of leeway on both ends of your stay. But once you get here you will discover a hiking paradise.

SIGHTSEEING

14 FURNA

Brava's port village Furna (pop. 600) lies at the mouth of a valley in the north-east of the island. Nestled beneath a concrete rainwater reservoir there are white, blue and grey buildings around the natural bay formed in a crater that was flooded by the sea. The harbour is the only permanent point of access to the island and is protected by towering walls of rock on three sides. A surfaced road winds its way up to Nova Sintra 7km away. The steep 4km-long footpath up the mountain is shorter and more attractive. *F17*

15 NOVA SINTRA ★

Brava's capital Nova Sintra (pop. 1,500) lies 500m above the sea on a fertile plane that is often engulfed in fog. The pleasantly temperate climate led the colonial administrators of Fogo and Santiago to build summer residences here in the 18th and 19th centuries. This resulted in the development of a charming little town with wide streets laid out like a chessboard that was named "new Sintra" after its Portuguese model Sintra.

The main street is lined with what

were once elegant mansions; trees and flowers grow between the wrought-iron lanterns on the central reservation. The main streets meet at the park-like *Praça Eugénio Tavares*. This is also where you will find the *town hall*, a modern *Nazarene church* and the *music pavilion*. A plaster model shows the relief of the island, and in Europe the old manual water pump would have long become a museum piece.

The musician and poet Eugénio Tavares (1867–1930) was born in Nova Sintra and was one of the pioneering artists in Cape Verde culture. He composed songs for local people with texts in Kriolu. He also criticised the Portuguese colonial rulers to an extent that, in 1900, he had to flee into exile to the United States. It was only when the Republic was proclaimed ten years later that he was able to return to his island. Many song lyrics of melancholic *mornas* can be traced back to Tavares. He was the island's best-known citizen and he married the daughter of wealthy merchants and lived in the house which is now the 🐦 *Museu de Eugénio Tavares (Mon–Sat, irregular opening hours | admission free | Rua da Cultura | ⏱ 30 mins)*. An interesting collection of exhibits gives you an insight into the life of the wealthy upper classes in the 19th century. A small garden with flowers planted in the shape of a guitar reminds you of the musical gifts of this highly talented man. In front of the house, a statue shows him seated, holding a sheet bearing the words of the island's beautiful hymn, one of his own compositions. His baptismal church *Igreja São João Baptista* is located on the eastern outskirts of town.

Nearby, a stone replica of Columbus' ship *Santa Maria* awaits St John the Baptist's Day when the townspeople celebrate the island's biggest festival, the *Festa de São João*, at the monument. *F17*

16 FONTE DE VINAGRE

The Fonte de Vinagre (Vinegar Spring) lies in a wide valley below Nova Sintra. The water contains fluoride and bicarbonate and tastes slightly sour. It is said that the water has curative properties and in times gone by the ill used to come here to bathe. There are terracotta heads with their mouths wide open on the four corners of the old 19th-century *bathhouse*. A paved path leads down to the spring from Santa Bárbara. *F17*

17 JOÃO D'NOLE/MATO GRANDE

The two villages of João d'Nole and Mato Grande (pop. 400) are located a little way above Nova Sintra. João d'Nole is a very picturesque little hamlet with well-cared-for houses and many orchards. The *Igreja Santo Antão*, a small, turquoise-coloured church, stands on a rise. Mato Grande is not quite as idyllic as its sister village but makes up for this with spectacular views over the entire east coast. *F17*

18 NOSSA SENHORA DO MONTE

The village (pop. 150) is tucked up on a mountain ridge in the north-western section of the central hilly country. The church stands on a large square with a view of the Fajã Valley. The road leading here passes through the village of *Cova Joana* where you will be able to admire some magnificent colonial mansions. *F17*

19 FAJÃ D'ÁGUA ★

This harbour village (pop. 300) is in a rocky bay that was formed by a flooded volcano crater and used to be important for whaling. Bizarre black rocks tower up out of the crystal-clear turquoise water. There is only room for a handful of houses in the area between the dark pebble beach and the massive mountain; most of them stand in a row along the shore. Tattered coconut and date palms sway in the wind. There is a turquoise-coloured church at the northern entrance to the village. The beach is not suitable for swimming but there are some natural seawater pools in the rocks 1km to the south. *F17*

EATING & DRINKING

O CASTELO

This *residêncial* and restaurant owned by former North American emigrants offers a good standard and delicious dishes. The owner speaks English. *Daily | Nova Sintra | Zona Castelo | tel. 2 85 10 63 | €€*

ESPLANADA SODADE

Sit on the terrace of the restaurant's pavilion in the middle of the main square, which is covered in flowers, and experience local life at close range: school children on their way

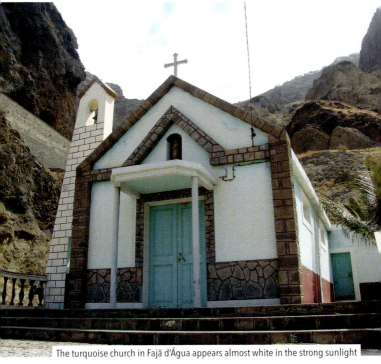

The turquoise church in Fajã d'Água appears almost white in the strong sunlight

home, housewives doing the shopping, town hall staff during their lunch break ... *Daily, Sun only in the evening | Nova Sintra | Praça Eugénio Tavares | tel. 9 95 97 18 | €*

LUANDA
Everything deliciously fresh from the barbecue: fish either filleted or whole, chicken, chicken thigh, cutlets and more. There is little variety available on Brava, but here you can also get a burger or vegetable platter. Pleasant service and reliable opening hours. *Daily | Nova Sintra | south of the main square | tel. 2 85 24 69 | €*

POR DO SOL
A bar-restaurant on the main square with a few small tables outside – perfect for people-watching. Good-value lunch menu, fish and meat from the barbecue. Interesting in the evenings, too, when locals drop in for a glass of *grogue* or *pontche*. *Daily | Nova Sintra | Praça Eugénio Tavares | no telephone | €*

SHOPPING

MINI-MERCADO POUPANÇA
Shopping off the beaten track is not that easy on Brava. However, this

INSIDER TIP
Best shopping on Brava

brand-new super-market has everything from food and drinks to shoes and hygiene products. *Nova Sintra | Rua Sossego*

SPORT & ACTIVITIES

BATHING

INSIDER TIP
In between the rocks

Brava does not have a bathing beach. The only chance of a swim is in the *sea swimming pools* near Fajã d'Água. A stairway south of the village leads down to a handful of rock pools with warm water (and a few sea urchins!). If the surf is strong, the waves smash against the rocks – sometimes so violently that it is impossible to swim here too.

HIKING

Many old donkey trails – some of them paved and most in good condition – criss-cross the highlands. Although Brava is the epitome of a hiking island, hikers are few and far between – the island is too remote and difficult to reach. There is no sign-posting and it is essential that you always have a map of the area or a GPS with you.

A lovely three-hour hike along donkey trails takes you from the mountains down to the Atlantic. The path starts at the *Igreja Nossa Senhora do Monte* and winds its way to Lavadura. There, you go over to the right side of the slope and start your descent to Lagoa. You can either cover the last third by going back along the

bottom of the valley or – a bit longer – through the village. The mango trees and coconut palms along the old irrigation channels provide some shade. You then pass through a steep cleft in the valley back to the main path.

From *Nova Sintra* to the *Fonte de Vinagre* is a pleasant walk that takes about 90 minutes and starts at the "Santa Maria" memorial in Vila Nova

Sintra. A steep path directly behind it leads a few hundred feet downhill, until it meets the new road and continues on the other side – always downhill – first to Santa Bárbara and finally to the spring. If you find the entire stretch too strenuous, you can cover the last section on the road – it is a little longer but not as steep.

NIGHTLIFE

If you want to know where to spend the evening in Nova Sintra, ask on the Praça Eugénio Tavares in the centre. Almost all the relevant restaurants are close by: just listen to where the music is coming from!

Bathing fun in the rock pools at Fajã d'Água

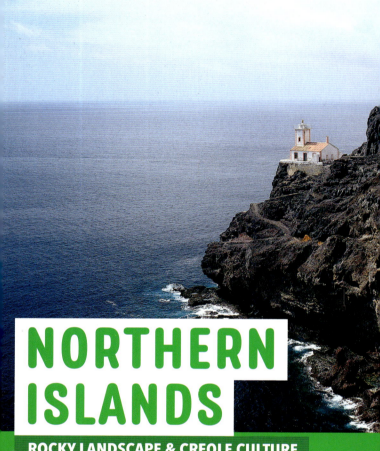

NORTHERN ISLANDS

ROCKY LANDSCAPE & CREOLE CULTURE

Mighty rocks rise up almost vertically out of the ocean. Battered by the wind and weather, deep, eroded valleys open up into the Atlantic; jagged gullies split the sand-polished slopes and bottomless ravines yawn between the gigantic rocks.

The almost 2,000m-high mountains dominate the appearance of the northern islands. They – and the wind – determine where there will be enough water, where fruit and vegetables can flourish, where people can live. The mountains on São Nicolau and Santo Antão are high

A marvellous lookout, but the track to the São Vicente lighthouse is too dangerous to walk

enough to stop the clouds blown in by the trade winds; on their north sides there are fertile green valleys where tropical fruit, vegetables and sugar cane grow. There could be no greater contrast to the landscape on the other side of the peaks where there is nothing but brown desert.

Santo Antão and São Nicolau are perfect for indepndent tourists and hikers as well as being a centre of Creole art and literature, while São Vicente attracts visitors with the lively and musical metropolis of Mindelo.

NORTHERN ISLANDS

Ponta do Sol ★ `5`
Cruzinha
Coculi
`4` **Ribeira Grande** ★
36km, 1 hr
Delgadim ★ `3`
`6` Cidade das Pombas
Ribeira do Paúl ★ `7`
`2` Cova do Paúl
Manta Velha
Ribeira da Cruz
Lagoa
Pico da Cruz
Ribeira da Aguda
Jorge Luiz
Chã d'Orgueiro
Santo Antão
p.96
Cirio
Chã de Morte
Lagedos
`1` Porto Novo
Praia de Tarrafal
de Monte Trigo
Ponta Sul
`8` Tarrafal de Monte Trigo
1 hr
Canal de São Vicente
Salamansa
Baía
das Gatas
Praia de Laginha
Mindelo ★ `9`
Lamejão
`12` Monte Verde
Calhau `11`
10km, 10 mins
São Pedro `10`
São Vicente
p.104
Praia de São Pedro
2 hrs

OCEANO
ATLÂNTICO

OCEANO

ATLÂNTICO

SANTO ANTÃO

(*B-D 2–4*) **Santo Antão's lifeblood is the road. And that is no surprise if you consider these mountains! They soar vertically skywards with rugged, eroded valleys and dizzying precipices to the left and right.**

Constructing a road in this terrain is a real adventure. The surfaced road across the island was built 50 years ago and the route along the eastern coast was completed in 2008. The most beautiful of all the routes in Cape Verde leads from Porto Novo, where you arrive on the island, 1,400m uphill and back down the other side diagonally across the island to its capital Ribeira Grande. That is the starting point of the road – a remarkable feat of engineering – that runs north-west along the coast to Ponta do Sol (5km) and south to Cidade das Pombas and onwards to Porto Novo. Sugar cane cultivation is the main source of income. In the landscape you'll see sugar presses and distilleries, evidence of what becomes of the tall, slender canes: the famous *grogue* of Santa Antão – it is said to be the archipelago's best, and the export of sugar cane liquor is as vital today as it ever was. Individual tourism is becoming increasingly important, especially for those who are keen hikers and Santo Antão is an ideal destination for this activity. The 1,979m-high *Tope de Coroa* is Cape Verde's second highest mountain (after the Pico do Fogo). Old, paved mule tracks wind their way all over the mountainous 779-km² island. The 1,170m-high Cova do Paúl in the north-east highlands has an impressive crater with a diameter of 800m. The tropical Ribeira do Paúl valley runs down from this peak to the ocean.

SIGHTSEEING

1 PORTO NOVO

The harbour town of Porto Novo (pop. 12,000) is located in the south-eastern part of the island. This is where the ferries from Mindelo arrive in the morning and afternoon. A paved road leads from the harbour to the centre of town where colourful fishing boats lie in the shade of a few acacias on the small beach with black sand. In spite of its importance as a port and as the largest settlement on Santo Antão, Porto Novo's tourist appeal is only gradually increasing; most visitors take one of the waiting ⚑ *aluguers* and head off for the other side of the island as soon as they arrive. *D3*

2 COVA DO PAÚL

In clear weather, you will have a fantastic view to the north-east over the entire length of the Ribeira do Paúl all the way from the rim of the crater down to the Atlantic. The panorama is especially impressive when the clouds swirl over the jagged edge into the crater. *D2*

3 DELGADIM ★

On the old, paved road between Porto Novo and Ribeira Grande lies a spectacular narrow section. On the right and left of the road, the cliffs fall almost vertically for hundreds of metres into the depths. On one side, you can look down to Ribeira Grande, on the other, Ribeira da Torre, Ribeira de Duque and the impressive rock face of Orgãos. *D2*

4 RIBEIRA GRANDE ⭐

The island's capital lies in the estuary of the two valleys of Ribeira Grande and Ribeira da Torre. The town (pop. 11,000) is a bustling meeting place for locals and tourists alike with its wide selection of shops, restaurants and guesthouses. The *Avenida 5 de Julho* leads into town and is lined with pastel-coloured merchant houses in various stages of renovation – or decay. The heart of the town is the main square *Praça Nossa Senhora do Rosário* with the Catholic church. The narrow side streets with their uneven cobblestones lead from there to a labyrinth of narrow, winding lanes with small shops and workshops. *D2*

5 PONTA DO SOL ⭐

Ponta do Sol (pop. 2,100) is located on a flat promontory in the extreme north – the northernmost point in the entire archipelago. Two roads lead down from the main square to the small harbour ⚑ *Boca de Pistola* that is somewhat protected by a makeshift breakwater. Since the foundation of Porto Novo, it has only been used by fishermen. It is also a meeting place, e.g. for playing *oril*. The renovated yellow *town hall* (1882), the former *infirmary* with a massive flight of steps leading up to it, and the Catholic *church* with its two towers on the sides, are all in the centre of town around a spacious square. Ponta do Sol is a pleasantly quiet little town where holidaymakers can still find everything they need. *D2*

6 CIDADE DAS POMBAS

On the north coast, 10km from Ribeira Grande, is Cidade das Pombas (pop. 2,000). This is the main town in the Paúl district and it lies at the mouth of the Ribeira do Paúl where it runs into the sea. Steep cliffs extend down to the bay and its narrow pebble beach. Black stones, the size of a human head are ground down by the fierce

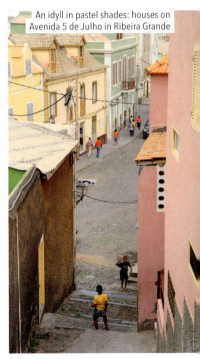

An idyll in pastel shades: houses on Avenida 5 de Julho in Ribeira Grande

breakers. The strong current makes it dangerous to bathe here. Behind the single colourful row of houses coconut palms rustle in the wind. The public buildings are in the east of the town: the *church*, built in 1885, the *town hall* and the health centre. On a hill above the city, the *statue* of the town's saint, Santo António, keeps watch over the people.

Next to the petrol station, the sugar cane press in the 🏴 *Trapiche Ildo Benrós (daily 9am–4pm | admission 100 CVE)* under the mighty almond tree is 400 years old and still in operation! It provides the raw material for the *grogue* and various other liqueurs (passion fruit has a lovely tropical flavour) which you can taste and buy on

site. ==Sugar cane is pressed between January and April/May in the traditional way using a pair of oxen: it's fascinating to watch!== *D2*

🟩 RIBEIRA DO PAÚL ⭐

This is the greenest place in Cape Verde: huge mango and breadfruit trees provide shade and whisper in the wind, and every inch of the ground is covered with vegetables and sugar cane as well as coconut palms, papaya and banana trees. The valley winds its way (6km) from the Cova crater down to the Atlantic – a drop in altitude of about 1,000m! There is so much to see: cloud forests full of lichens, banana and coffee plantations, palm groves and fields of sugar cane swaying in the breeze and the abundant water gushing through

the streams, reservoirs and canals throughout the year. The village *Passagem* is almost in the centre where an old, decaying swimming pool is hidden in a shady oasis under blue jacaranda and pink bougainvillea bushes. *D2*

🟩 TARRAFAL DE MONTE TRIGO

On the west side of Santo Antão is the wide bay (10km) of Tarrafal de Monte Trigo (pop. 1,000). If you want to visit this lush, green paradise, you will have to put up with a two-hour journey along an adventurous track. Once there, you will be rewarded for your efforts with ideal bathing conditions at the black lava sand beach. The sea is usually calm because the high mountains protect the bay from the wind. It's a place to relax and enjoy nature. *B3*

EATING & DRINKING

A BEIRA MAR

Donna Fátima serves two excellent daily specials at an unbeatable price. *Daily | Ponta do Sol | Rua Central | tel. 2 25 10 08 | €*

CANTINHO DE AMIZADE

This restaurant has enjoyed a fine reputation for years and so have its prices. Enjoy fish and seafood, salads, omelettes and spaghetti in the snack bar, the restaurant or on the lovely, shady patio. *Mon–Sat | Ribeira Grande | Rua Padre Fernando Barreto | tel. 2 21 13 92 | €*

High mountains and blue sea: Santo Antão offers both

CASA MARACUJA

The Casa Maracuja in Cidade das Pombas is designed to make you happy: with tasty Cape Verdean specialities, home-made juice and liqueurs (try the passion fruit!), tourist information and expert hiking tips, the fabulous views from the shady rooftop terrace and frequent live music. Feeling happy already? *Daily | Cidade das Pombas | tel. 2 23 10 00 | FB | €€*

O CURRAL

Edible flowers: yellow and orange nasturtiums decorate the very best salad in Cape Verde. Home-grown organic vegetables with olive oil and home-made sugar cane vinegar are a vitamin boost. Many other specialities (cheese, bread, spreads, dips, fruit juices, etc.) are equally delicious. *Closed in the evening | Cidade das Pombas | Chã de João Vaz | tel. 2 23 12 13 | €*

DIVIN' ART

The atmosphere here is all art and aesthetics. Literature, music or painting, arts and crafts, tradition and history, poetry or culinary delights are very much the focus, and when some of the owners' artist friends gather in the evening, the creativity reaches even loftier heights. On Fridays, communal entertainment is on the cards and, if you can recite a poem or join in with the music, you will be a welcome guest! *Daily | João Dias | Ribeira Grande | tel. 9 99 57 73 | divinart.cv | €–€€*

A drink at one of Ponta do Sol's restaurants also buys you a free view of local daily life

O VELEIRO
Freshly caught fish served above the roaring Atlantic with great harbour views. Regional cuisine, pizza and excellent coffee. *Daily | Ponta do Sol | at the harbour | €€*

SHOPPING

CHEZ SANDRO
At the top of the Ribeira do Paúl, Sandro sells arts and crafts, but the real selling point is the Arabica coffee from the surrounding plantations. Take a break and taste it: it has been brewed in the traditional way. The home-made liqueurs from local *grogue* are just as delicious – try one with your coffee. *Cabo da Ribeira*

CREAJADE
Kim makes beautiful necklaces, earrings and other jewellery from colourful gemstones and clay beads which she produces by hand. Pretty small items or eye-catching bling: they are all attractive! *Ponta do Sol | Rua Central*

a wetsuit and abseil down one of nine gorges, up to 18m deep, some with flow-

INSIDER TIP
For adrenaline junkies...

ing water, under the expert guidance of Olivier Gilabert *(Pé La No Ar | Ponta do Sol | tel. 9 97 71 64 | pelanoar@gmail.com)*. Jumping, sliding, abseiling: canyoning gives you a tremendous adrenaline rush, and afterwards a traditional lunch will restore your strength.

DIVING

If you go diving or snorkelling off the coast of Tarrafal, you will not only encounter colourful fish, langoustines and eels, but with bit of luck perhaps also a manta ray or a turtle! Professional diver David *(Santo Antão Scuba Diving | Tarrafal | tel. 9 51 42 66 | caboverdescubadiving.com)* takes even complete novices on his fascinating dives.

HIKING

Santo Antão provides a wide range of hiking routes at all levels of difficulty. Deep gorges, tropical valleys, the steep coast, forests and volcanic landscapes allow for demanding ascents, as well as leisurely strolls. You can hike along the well-preserved donkey paths without a guide; these include the easy hike *from Cruzinha to Ponta do Sol*. It takes around five hours and leads uphill and down again for 12km along the coast with a difference in altitude of a good 500m. After you leave Cruzinha, continue in a westerly direction and follow the path past the football pitch and bizarre eroded

GENUINE

Franziska creates accessories such as hats, cushion covers and tablecloths, as well as dresses, skirts and trousers from colourful Senegalese wax prints. She can even sew tailormade items on request. *Ponta do Sol | Rua Central*

SPORT & ACTIVITIES

CANYONING

Experience a real adventure on Santo Antão: canyoning. Brave souls put on

rocks that lead to the steep zigzag descent to the abandoned village of Aranhas. Thereafter, the cliff path leads to the small village of Forminguinhas and then on to Corvo, where you can buy cold drinks and use the toilet in the *Pontinha de Giada*. You then continue hiking to the hamlet of *Fontainhas* – high up on a rock ledge – before reaching your destination, Ponta do Sol.

The more complicated routes should only be tackled by experienced hikers, and guides are essential in the isolated, western plateau! They will both show you the way and provide insights into life in Cape Verde.

If you are an animal lover, why not go on a 🐵 *donkey hike (Casa Espongeiro, see p. 101)*. Only suitable for children, but the donkeys will carry any baggage (up to 40kg). Get a local guide and one or two donkeys and explore the mountains of Santo Antão on the old mule tracks.

KAYAKING & SUP
When the sea in the bay of Tarrafal is sufficiently calm, you can paddle seated or standing up. Hire a kayak at *Marina d'Tarrafal (Tarrafal | tel. 2 27 60 78 | FB)* or a SUP board at *Santo Antão Scuba Diving (see above)* and have fun!

MOUNTAIN BIKING
Next to *Casa Espongeiro*, at an altitude

INSIDER TIP
... & mountain bikers

of 1,370m near the Cova crater, you can ==hire mountain bikes including all the necessary accessories== from the owner,

Alain *(Espongeiro | tel. 9 81 15 26 | casaespongeiro.com)*. You then ride back downhill on your bike, or accompany Alain, a passionate biker, on a tour through the incredible mountain scenery. Transfer of bikes to other towns can be arranged here, as can hiking with a donkey.

BEACHES
Santo Antão's coast is rugged with steep cliffs, rocks and reefs and it is equally rough underwater. Strong currents and heavy surf make swimming dangerous; there are only a few beaches for inexperienced swimmers.

In the Ribeira do Paúl you can hike through coffee and sugar cane plantations

PRAIA DE ESCORALET

There are three small bays with black-sand beaches approx. 25 minutes' walk from Porto Novo. Very popular with families at weekends because children can swim safely. *D3*

PRAIA DE TARRAFAL DE MONTE TRIGO

The long crescent-shaped sand-and-pebble beach below the village of Tarrafal de Monte Trigo is a real beauty. You can admire the colourful fishing boats and the fish that are spread on the stones to dry in the sun. Have a look at the fishermen's catch, go swimming or snorkelling or just relax.

Hopefully, this idyll is going to last because parts of it are already being modernised. *B3–4*

WELLNESS

SAN BAOBAB MASSAGE

Have you done too much walking or feel tense or tired? Rafaelle, a natural health professional and expert in traditional Chinese medicine, uses massage and acupressure to harmonise your energy system. *Tarrafal | tel. 9 72 51 71 | FB: Raphaelle.Galtier24*

FESTIVALS

NHÔ SAN JON

In the Porto Novo district, the statue of Saint João is carried by strong men from one village to the next over a four-week period. On 24 June it finally arrives in the capital, Porto Novo, where it is by then accompanied by a procession of many hundreds of people as well as drumming bands, drink sellers and – not to forget – a dozen local Catholic dignitaries. In the meantime, thousands of visitors have arrived because after the church service a big and rather more wordly party begins. Naturally, the saint must be celebrated in style ...

NIGHTLIFE

CANTINHO DE GATO PRETO

This cosy little restaurant is not exactly cheap, but the food is very good. Tourists love it because of the live music – so don't forget your dancing shoes! *Sun–Fri | Ponta do Sol*

SÃO VICENTE

(🗺 *D–E 4–5*) **Almost 95% of São Vicente's 80,000 inhabitants are in Mindelo. The city is the capital and lifeblood of the island; there is not much going on elsewhere. The few people who have made their home in Baia das Gatas, Calhau and São Pedro live an isolated life for the most part. People from town only liven up the village** streets and beach bars when they come here to relax and to have a good time at the weekend.

The 227km² of land is as dry as Cape Verde's desert islands; even the highest peak *(Monte Verde 774m)* is not high enough to stop the moisture-laden clouds of the trade wind. Outside Mindelo, there is not much more than brownish-red mountains and wide, desert-like valleys where hardly anything grows. This is why São Vicente was settled much later than the other islands. Although the sheltered harbour was often used by pirates as a hiding place, the first settlement was only established in 1794. There are idyllic small beach bays with fine white sand from the Sahara on the south-west and east coasts – too dangerous for bathing but great for a walk.

SIGHTSEEING

🟩 MINDELO ⭐

Mindelo is the second largest city (after Praia) in Cape Verde. The 4km-wide bay of a sunken volcano crater protects the large – but still

WHERE TO START?

Start in the centre of Mindelo where you find all the interesting sights in close proximity and a large selection of cafés for when you need a break. The *Rua Lisboa* and the *Avenida Amílcar Cabral* form the axis of the city, around which all the sights are arranged.

picturesque – town. The *Fortim d'el Rei* fortress is enthroned on a hill above; the *Monte Cara*, a rock that wind and weather have eroded and now resembles a human face (*cara* is Portuguese for face), stands guard in the west.

Flashy jeeps and designer sunglasses are testament to the town's rapidly growing middle class which includes well-dressed office workers and small business owners. The harbour area attracts all those with hopes – hopes for high profits, a job or even just money for the next *grogue*. Around 150 years ago, British immigrants, Creole slaves and sailors from all over the world flooded into the rapidly growing boom town and created a dynamic, cosmopolitan mixture. This was due to the coal trade which secured the provisioning of ships on the colonial Atlantic routes. Bars and a red-light district sprung up creating a special kind of culture with the unique music styles such as *morna* and *coladeira*. The musical and architectural heritage from that era established Mindelo's reputation as Cape Verde's cultural metropolis today.

Nowhere else on the Cape Verde Islands are there as many colonial buildings. Magnificent government buildings and stuccoed mansions line the shady squares and the broad *Avenida Amílcar Cabral* that runs along the shore. There is even a smaller version of Lisbon's Torre de Belém, dating from 1918, and, next door, the fish market with plenty of hustle and bustle among the stands with their silvery fish and exotic seafood. Women selling fish, fruit and

The music metropolis of Mindelo also produces instruments

The stone statue in front of the Torre de Belém is Cape Verde explorer Diogo Afonso

vegetables, sweets and cigarettes can also be seen across the street. Not far away is the 🌡 *Centro Cultural de Mindelo (Mon-Fri 9am-9pm, Sat 10am-12.30pm & 5-9pm, Sun 5-9pm | FB: CCMindelo)*, with an arts and crafts shop, a bookshop, a current painting or photography exhibition and a shady place to rest during the day. In the evening there is often music or theatre *(mindelact.org)*, book launches, lectures, cinema shows, etc.

Well-established – and sometimes old-fashioned – guesthouses and chic new hotels welcome their guests on the commercial street *Avenida 5 de Julho*. It leads to the *Praça Nova*, the most popular place to take a stroll in Mindelo. In the evening, people get together on the paths in the park

around an ornate art nouveau pavilion to see and be seen, and on Sundays local families promenade in all their finery to the music of a brass band.

Rua Lisboa is the heartbeat of the city with numerous small cafés and shops and already plenty of activity in the morning. In the historic market hall you can look down on mountains of fruit and vegetables from the upper gallery with its shops and bars. The *town hall* (1873), *Nossa Senhora da Luz* church (1863) and the pink, classical *Governor's Palace* are all just a few steps away.

🚩 Up until a few years ago, *Ribeira Bote* was one of the most deprived areas of Mindelo. Today visitors are shown through this part of town on guided walks in an effort to integrate

INSIDER TIP
Art & daily life

that particular community. You will get to know colourfully painted corrugated-iron shacks, creative wall art, artisans at work and real Mindelo life. Your guides are trained residents *(tel. 9 70 60 35 | FB: Ribeira Bote-Turismo Comunitário)* from Ribeira Bote.

The difference between nostalgic colonial style and the mirror façades of the new buildings is just one of many contrasts. The marked contrast between rich and poor is ever apparent in Mindelo: the business mogul with his luxurious yacht rubs shoulders with the shoe shiner. The growing middle class observes all of this with cosmopolitan sangfroid. *D4*

🔟 SÃO PEDRO

A handful of small, cube-shaped, pastel-coloured houses, a bar and a couple of shops: São Pedro (pop. 800) is a peaceful, languorous fishing village. It is located below two mountain flanks on the south-west coast only a stone's throw from the airport. Depending on the wind and weather, the ⚐ white sandy beach offers great conditions for speed surfing and swimming although sometimes it's only good for a walk. In strong wind, even the short walk to the lighthouse at the other end of the beach can be hazardous! *D4*

1️⃣1️⃣ CALHAU

The sleepy village of Calhau (pop. 450) is 18km south-east of Mindelo. It comes alive at weekends when visitors have fun on the beach during the day and then in the bars and restaurants in the evening. However, there are some proper highlights such as a rock pool formed by the small volcano at the end of the village, including a ladder to get in and out. Also, a few kilometres away, is the relatively "young" *Viana* volcano (approx. a 15-minute walk to the top) as well as the small, deserted beaches of *Boca da Lapa* and *Sandy Beach*. Make sure that you take sun protection! *E4*

1️⃣2️⃣ MONTE VERDE

On a clear day, the panoramic view of Mindelo's harbour bay from the summit is magnificent. It is also often possible to see as far as Santo Antão and the uninhabited islands of *Santa Luzia*, *Branco* and *Razo*. After leaving Mindelo, travel about 5km towards Baía das Gatas where there is a turn-off to the *Monte Verde Nature Reserve*. The road leads up to the plateau in a series of wide curves – you can drive, but it is far better to walk. *D4*

EATING & DRINKING

CARAVELA

This is about as good as it gets: sitting in the wooden pavilion on Laginha town beach with an ice-cold drink, looking out to the iridescent blue sea and watching the bathers ... *Daily | Mindelo | Laginha | tel. 2 32 29 27 | FB | €*

CHAVE D'OURO

Nostalgic charm on the first floor of the guesthouse of the same name. The food is reasonably priced and the fish is particularly good. *Daily | Mindelo | Alto São Nicolau | Av. 5 de Julho | tel. 2 32 70 50 | €*

CHEZ LUTCHA CALHAU
A popular place for an amazing Sunday buffet lunch (including seafood) for approx. 100 guests. Eventually, after everything has been cleared off the tables, including the dessert buffet, the 🚩 dancing begins. Join in – it's great fun! The restaurant is in the hamlet of Calhau, and they offer a free shuttle service from Mindelo *(departure 12.30pm, return 4.30pm | Restaurant Chez Lutcha). Tel. 2 32 16 36 | €€*

FRESKO FOOD BOUTIQUE
The place for vegans, vegetarians and lovers of fruit and vegetables where you find smoothies, juices, salads, herbal teas and other dishes prepared with fresh produce! They also offer chicken or ham sandwiches and a cup of coffee to go with your detox juice. *Mon–Sat | Mindelo | Rua António Aurélio Gonçalves | tel. 3 53 31 36 | FB | €*

GALERIA ZERO POINT ART
A large painting exhibition in the gallery on the ground floor plus culinary delicacies and live music every Thursday and Friday evening. *Wed–Mon in the evening | Mindelo | Rua Unidade Africana 62 | FB: zero pointart | €€*

HOTEL FOYA BRANCA 🏨
Spend a day by the sea and enjoy the lavish lunchtime buffet at this 4-star hotel: walk on the beach, explore the fishing village, sunbathe by the (children's) pool, swim, surf, dive ... *Admission incl. buffet 1,800 CVE (16.50€), children half price | São Pedro | tel. 2 30 74 00 | foyabranca. com*

PASTELARIA BETTENCOURT 🚩
This is where the locals come to eat: daily lunch specials and everything is tasty and inexpensive. Come early; it is always packed after 1pm! *Mon–Sat | Mindelo | Av. da República 27 | tel. 2 31 28 44 | €*

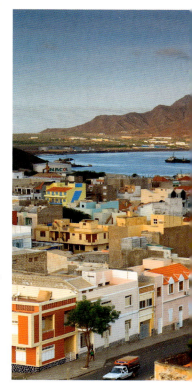

LA PERGOLA

Having escaped the hustle and bustle of Mindelo, here you can relax on recycled wooden furniture between arts and crafts and lush green plants. Enjoy a cold drink and an original Creole/French dish – welcome to the terrace of the French Cultural Centre! *Mon–Sat at lunchtime | Mindelo | Rua de Santo António 1 | tel. 9 31 13 19 | €*

SANTO ANDRÉ

Despite the long drive from Mindelo, people always return to eat here in the relaxing atmosphere of the shady courtyard where fabulous food is served in person by the likeable proprietor. After a large lunch you can take a walk on the long, white sandy beach of São Pedro! *Tue–Sun | São Pedro | opposite the Hotel Foya Branca | tel. 2 31 51 00 & 9 71 17 65 | €€*

SHOPPING

CAPVERTDESIGN + ARTESANATO

This amazing shop has something for everyone in an enormous unique collection of both traditional and

The sun illuminates Mindelo's houses one last time before disappearing over the horizon

innovative arts and crafts from all Cape Verde Islands. Furniture and decorative items, artwork by the *rabelados* and other artists, household goods and books, Cape Verdean delicacies, etc. Have you ever seen jewellery made from sand?

INSIDER TIP
Wearable sand

Beads are made from sand, for example, white from São Vicente or black from Santo Antão, and then combined with high-quality semi-precious stones to create earrings, necklaces and bangles. *Mindelo | Rua da Luz | FB*

HARMONIA

All that Cape Verde has to offer in the field of music: advice is given and you can listen before you buy your CDs with every kind and style of Cape Verdean music. *Mindelo | Edifício Benfica, close to the town hall*

SPORT & ACTIVITIES

WATER SPORTS

Mindelo boasts the only marina (145 berths) in Cape Verde *(marina-mindelo.com)*. If you don't have your own boat, you can charter a yacht or take part in a sailing trip *(tel. 2 32 67 72 and 9 91 58 78 | boatcv.com, trend-travel-yachting.com)*. The *Praia do São Pedro (🔲 D4)* is only suitable for swimming when the sea is calm but it is a great diving spot. Pros know the bay as a speedsurfing hotspot *(kapverdensurf.com, short.travel/kav11)* because the two mountain ranges, which run parallel to the prevailing winds, produce a gigantic funnel effect. From mid-October to mid-May you can reach speeds of 20–30 knots here! Kite- and windsurfing are also possible on the beach near the fishing village of Salamansa where kitesurfing instructor Jaír *(tel. 9 57 75 29 | FB: kitesurfsalamansa)* offers courses and the required equipment. In the same location you'll also find *Kitesurf Cabo Verde (kitesurfcaboverde.com)*, another operator which aims at involving local people in kite tourism.

INSIDER TIP
Feeling the need for speed?

BEACHES

BAÍA DAS GATAS

The "bay of cats" is the most popular bathing beach on São Vicente. Every year in August, tens of thousands of people make a pilgrimage to the Festival Baía das Gatas. Protected by volcanic rocks that reach down to the sea, the semi-circular bay forms a wide, sheltered lagoon which is great for families. The sea remains shallow a long way from the beach; swimmers can dive into the cool water from a long stone breakwater. 🔲 E4

PRAIA DE LAGINHA

In the early morning, you can look for shells, jog or swim on the beautiful Mindelo city beach pretty much on your own because bathers tend to turn up later in the day. However, make sure that you don't leave any valuables lying around unattended! *Shoreline road to the ferry port, then another 500m on foot | 🔲 D4*

It doesn't look like it here, but São Pedro beach is popular with speedsurfers

PRAIA DO NORTE & PRAIA GRANDE

These two beaches are south of the Baía das Gatas in a bay that stretches as far as the Calhau promontory. Perfect for sunbathing and walks along the beach, but the currents make swimming risky. *E4*

WELLNESS

Lean back and enjoy a facial from Roxana Lima (*Mamdyara | Mindelo | Rua Unidade Africana 58 | tel. 9 94 43 92*) from Argentina. She uses natural ingredients for all her treatments.

FESTIVALS

CARNIVAL ⚑

The Mindelo carnival is *the* event of the year, much looked forward to by local people. Rio de Janeiro doesn't seem far away when the samba dancers in their glittering glamourous costumes get going and fiery rhythms of the drums enrapture both the participants and spectators. The procession on Tuesday afternoon is pretty small, which means that it has to go round the main streets twice to make it worthwhile, but who cares? People dance, celebrate and drink. Be careful not to get too close to the *mandingas* who are painted all in black, otherwise you will get covered in paint yourself!

INSIDER TIP
Wet paint!

FESTIVAL BAÍA DAS GATAS 🐟

The Baía das Gatas music festival is another unforgettable event on São Vicente. On the first weekend in August after the full moon, tens of

A *noite caboverdeana* should be a part of your holiday in Cape Verde

thousands of people gather in the village of the same name 12km east of Mindelo. The stage directly by the beach hosts Cape Verdean, African, European and Latin-American musicians who produce the legendary atmosphere. Countless small stalls sell snacks and drinks. *FB*

MINDELACT

The country's most important theatre event attracts local and international artists from all corners of the globe and includes music, exhibitions, lectures, readings and workshops. In this way, November is the annual month of culture. *mindelact.org*

NIGHTLIFE

Nightlife in Mindelo means first and foremost live music! Great solo artists or bands play at the 🐦 *noites caboverdeanas* that accompany dinner in almost all restaurants on specific days. You can find out who is playing where from the hotels, tourist information office and flyers. The party continues in the discos – but only at the weekend! They are empty before midnight and only get really crowded between 2am and 3am. Please note that whatever the time or destination (apart from the city centre), you should never walk at night but always take a taxi.

In summer, the Laginha beach promenade is the city's noisy party mile with many interesting pubs – *e.g. Gabylandia, Bar Holanda, Ote Level* – all of which are packed with revellers. Below the Bar Caravela (see p. 108) next to the beach is the discotheque of the same name – popular with the young in-crowd!

LIVRARIA NHO DJUNGA

Once an insider tip, the tiny bookshop in Mindelo's live music quarter has become an institution. At the weekend, well-known local musicians perform, often accompanied by other artists and even guests. *Daily |*

Mindelo | Rua Senador Vera Cruz 82 | FB: NhoDjunga

MARINA FLOATING BISTRO

The Floating Bistro gently rocks on the waves in the marina. While hardy sea-farers barely notice the steady movement, even people who prefer terra firma seem to like it. Location: ring the bell next to the gated door at the end of the pier, then walk down the jetty for 30m and turn left. *Daily | Mindelo | Marina | FB*

METALO FAST GOOD

The Creole version of McDonald's produces burgers, baguettes, sandwiches, wraps, nuggets (fish or chicken), sauces, iced tea and more according to their own recipes and from local produce. They are intent on offering high-quality fast food! On top of that there is a stage for concerts by local artists. Worth visiting! *Closed at lunchtime | Mindelo | Largo da Praça José Lopes | tel. 9 96 20 20 | FB*

INSIDER TIP
Fast food & live music

PAVILHÃO

Not everyone likes a liqueur, some find it too sweet and sticky. However, Donna Jóia serves her guests the *stemperod*, a liqueur with *grogue* which tastes quite different and is rather strong. The favourite variety is *stemperod de tambarina* (tamarind). *Daily | Mindelo | Praça Nova*

SÃO NICOLAU

(*H–K 5–7*) **Many people regard São Nicolau as Santo Antão's smaller, somewhat unprepossessing sister.**

The island is not as big, the mountains not as high, the valleys not as deep, the coastline not as steep. But the 346-km² island does at least have an unusual shape: the outline of the west coast resembles that of the African continent while the eastern section is a long, narrow promontory. São Nicolau is still an insider tip and tourism is not as developed as it is on its larger sister island. There are only two towns of any size: the capital Ribeira Brava in the north-east and Tarrafal, the harbour town, in the south-west. That is where half of the island's 15,000 inhabitants live. The long, narrow eastern region is sparsely populated.

São Nicolau's mountains make it especially interesting for hikers and explorers and its beaches stretch for miles in the south-west. This is a combination unmatched by any of the other islands. The landscape in the south-west is dominated by dry, scorched land. The clouds remain on the north-eastern side of Monte Gordo (1,312m) and the surrounding mountain slopes where the foothills are

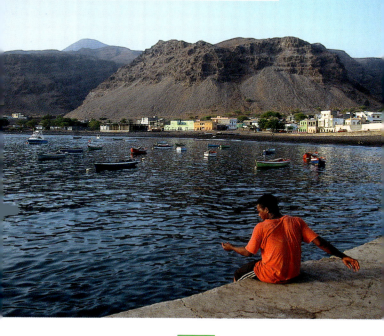

Tarrafal's harbour is used by fishing boats, cutters and cruise ships

green and fertile. Sugar cane, vegetables and tropical fruit grow there on the fertile lava soil of Fajã de São Nicolau.

SIGHTSEEING

13 TARRAFAL

Tarrafal (pop. 5,000) is the hottest place on São Nicolau. Everything revolves around the port. Fishing boats and cutters bring their catch to the shore and it is then processed in the cold stores and a fish factory. The fishing museum *Museu da Pesca (Mon–Sat 11am–3pm and 5–8pm | admission free | Av. Assis Cadório | ⏱ 30 mins)*, which opened in 2019, gives you an insight into tuna fishing in the past century, and the adjoining *restaurant (daily | €–€€)* not only serves excellent (fish) dishes but also has live music some evenings.

INSIDER TIP
Hungry? To the museum!

The ferry from Praia to Mindelo – and sometimes even a cruise ship – stops over. You will discover some charming buildings if you take a stroll through the centre of the town that is laid out in a grid pattern, and there are two sandy beaches that are great for bathing: one by the harbour, which is a pretty sight with the colourful boats, and the other at the *Praia d'Tedja*. 📖 H6

14 MONTE GORDO

The "fat mountain" is the highest on the island and is surrounded by the nature reserve of the same name. It is worth visiting for the many endemic plant and animal species, especially the common Dragon tree, one of the island's landmarks. A nature protection centre provides interesting information when it is open to visitors. The area around the mountain is great for walks and hikes. 📖 H6

15 RIBEIRA BRAVA ⭐

In 1693, the threat of pirates caused the residents of the coastal settlement of Porto da Lapa to leave their homes and establish Ribeira Brava further inland. Today's capital (pop. 7,000) lies at an altitude of 200m in a wide valley with a mighty riverbed. The colonial architecture is still present in the well-preserved merchant houses and the *Nossa Senhora do Rosário* cathedral. In 1866, a seminary was established in this diocesan town; for years it attracted the archipelago's greatest thinkers until the Portuguese government closed it in 1917. The building on Rua Seminário, on the south side of the river, was donated by Dr Júlio José Dias (1805–73); his bust has pride of place on the main square, the *Praça do Terreiro*. The small park is surrounded by the cathedral, the historic schoolhouse (today, the public library) and some two-storey colonial houses. There are many shops and workshops in the adjacent street as well as a handful of restaurants and guesthouses. An alley opposite the church leads to a small area of greenery in front of the post office (free WiFi) and from there visitors are only a few steps away from a park with plane and jacaranda trees next to the deeply eroded riverbed. 📖 H6

16 PREGUIÇA

The tranquil fishing village of Preguiça (pop. 600) on the east coast offers a magnificent view of the eastern semi-circle of the bay. A road leads down to the Atlantic and you will catch glimpses of yellow and blue tiled houses high above the sea. You will also see the harbour breakwater, the village church and colourful boats on the black beach. At the end of the quay are the ruins of the customs house that was built in 1890. The ruins of a fort – there are still some canons to be seen – and a monument to the discoverer of Brazil Pedro Alvares Cabral who dropped anchor here in the year 1500, are reminders of the historical importance of the village. *J6*

17 JUNCALINHO

The pretty village (pop. 400) is located on the northern side of the eastern headland. The small settlement with its traditional little houses is located in a picturesque position on a rocky coast. The *Capela da Sagrada Família* was constructed using natural stone in 1960. Only a few minutes' walk to the north-east of the village, you will find some pools in the rocks that are ideal for swimming. *J6*

18 CARBERINHO ⭐

One of the most beautiful places in the archipelago: the bizarre, eroded rocks and the raging surf create a spectacular sight. From Tarrafal drive towards Praia Branca until you see a water tank on the right and then, a few hundred feet further on the left, a signpost. Follow the tyre tracks and park your car at the top of the hill. You then hike down to the cliffs. The best way to do this trip is in a hired car with a driver. *H6*

19 PRAIA BRANCA

Ruby red, bottle green, aquamarine blue: this pretty village (pop. 500) with colourful houses nestles in the valley with steep, winding lanes and crooked steps and paths that lead to hidden corners and idyllic courtyards. *H6*

EATING & DRINKING

BELA SOMBRA DALILA 🚩

For dinner you must try the traditional dishes of São Nicolau, e.g. *modjo*, a vegetable stew with goat, but make sure you leave room for their desserts, which are heavenly. Excellent service. *Daily | Ribeira Brava | take the street on the right off the main square past the church | tel. 2 35 12 98 | €*

PADARIA MATIZINH

Where can you get great coffee, wholemeal bread *(pão integral)*, a delicious lunch *(prato do dia)* or a sandwich? In this bakery close to the post office and Câmara Municipal! *Mon–Sat 8.30am–6pm | Ribeira Brava*

SHOPPING

MERCADO MUNICIPAL

On the ground floor of the market hall you can find fresh fruit and vegetables, fish in the basement and a few boutiques on the top floor, e.g. *Joci's shop (No. 4)*, where they sell hand-sewn children's clothes, dolls and all kinds of accessories made from colourful wax prints. *Ribeira Brava*

SABORES DO CANTO

From a large variety of tropical fruit, the women's cooperative in Canto de Fajã makes delicious jams, liqueurs and fruit juices as well as hand-made soap with aloe vera and medicinal clay. You can buy their products in the markets, in a few shops or on site.

SPORT & ACTIVITIES

HIKING

São Nicolau offers many interesting mountain and coastal hikes. The is an incredible variety of landscapes on this island: fertile green forest areas alternate with barren mountain ranges without any vegetation and with dizzying, craggy coasts … *Toi D'Armanda (Kretcheu | Tarrafal | tel. 2 36 18 27 and 9 94 51 46 | FB: Kretcheu Lda)* is an experienced hiking guide who is not only very knowledgeable but also helps to organise everything you could possibly need: accommodation, transfers, excursions, etc.

Most hikers climb to the peak of *Monte Gordo* from Cachaço but don't know that they are missing Cape Verde's most beautiful hike by a few

Thatched roofs and stone walls are typical of the northern islands

Surf crashing onto high rocks at Carberinho: not for bathing, just for admiring

INSIDER TIP
Changing scenery

metres! ==The *circular track* around the highest mountain on São Nicolau from Falejão offers more varied and breathtaking scenery than any other hike.== It will take you five to six hours to climb through rugged gorges and up steep ascents, across gently rolling hills and through tropical valleys, wading through black volcanic ash and lava areas as well as crossing stony deserts and misty cloud forest. Plus there are great views of the wild ocean along the steep coastline.

Do not miss out on the incredible gorge of the ⭐ *Ribeira da Prata!* Inexperienced hikers are advised to approach it from Ribeira da Prata. Otherwise, this absolutely beautiful hike from *Canto de Fajã* requires a good level of fitness and a sense of direction: after ascending approx. 250m towards Assomada, the route takes you along several wide sweeps approx. 700m above Cruzinha and then goes steeply downhill to Ribeira da Prata.

BEACHES

There are lovely bathing beaches on the west coast of the island as well as in the bay in the south-east (*Carriçal, Preguiça*). Hardly any of them have ant shade and there's practically no infrastructure for tourists.

PRAIA BAIXO ROCHA 🌴 👯

Far and away the island's most beautiful beach, although it's a bit remote:

A hidden gem pale sand, turquoise sea and even a bit of shade between the rocks. To find it from Tarrafal, go towards the hospital, then it's signposted on the right. Approx. 8km. *H6*

PRAIA DE CARRIÇAL

Remotely located on the south-eastern coast is the pretty little village beach of Carriçal with black sand. Acacia trees offer their shade, coconut palms sway in the wind and colourful fishing boats bob up and down in the waves. *K6*

PRAIA GRANDE

Finally some shade! This is a welcome bonus at Praia Grande, where you get a beach of fine dark sand for cooling off in the sea. From Tarrafal drive in the direction of Praia Branca. *H6*

WELLNESS

FARINHA DE PAU

In good hands Sergio from Brazil is an expert in various relaxation methods and in making you feel healthy and happy: chiropractic Japanese Samurai style (Seitai), Ayurvedic massage or the almost forgotten traditional healing ways of São Nicolau. He uses sand with an extremely high mineral content to alleviate rheumatic and other ailments. His wife Simone gives facials using medicinal clay and other natural substances. *Praia Branca | tel. 9 15 39 16 | farinhadepau.com*

FESTIVALS

The carnival of São Nicolau is almost as famous as that on Mindelo but is celebrated on a smaller scale. Instead of pouring in the cash, here they employ creativity to make incredible costumes which are then presented in a lavish procession. It is said that the local carnival princes and princesses are the most beautiful, and the people certainly know how to throw a good party.

NIGHTLIFE

GOLFINHO

This maritime-themed café has a nice, shady terrace, where you can eat good, inexpensive meals during the day. And on Fridays and Saturdays, it's party time. The action starts late but carries on until the morning. *Daily | Tarrafal | Telha*

SILA

It is lovely to have lunch on the terrace, but in the evening there is even greater fun to be had: live music, dance parties with DJ or football on the big screen, plus ice-cold beers and delicious cocktails, Cape Verdean tapas and a great atmosphere. *Daily | Ribeira Brava | FB*

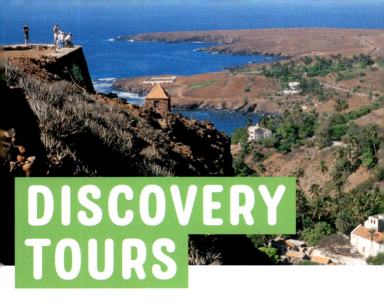

DISCOVERY TOURS

Do you want to get under the skin of these islands? Then our discovery tours provide the perfect guide – they include advice on which sights to visit, tips on where to stop for that perfect holiday snap, a choice of the best places to eat and drink, and suggestions for fun activities.

❶ SANTIAGO: JOURNEY BACK 500 YEARS

➤ Follow in the footsteps of Columbus and Francis Drake
➤ Discover a UNESCO World Heritage Site in Cape Verde's oldest town
➤ Hike through a lush and rugged tropical valley

📍	Praia	🏁	Sucupira
⇄	32km	🚶	8 hrs (4 hrs total walking time)
▁▂▃	Easy	↗	200m
ⓘ	The hike is a steep ascent from the start and goes over terrain with scree.		

PANORAMIC VIEWS OF HISTORY

Travel by taxi from ➊ Praia ➤ p. 70 to ➋ Fortaleza Real de São Filipe. In the information centre *(daily 9am–6pm | admission 500 CVE),* buy a ticket that gives you access to all the monuments on this tour and look around the fort while your taxi waits. You'll have a wonderful view from the top of the ramparts.

MARVEL AT THE BIRDS & THE TREES

The taxi now takes you to ➌ Calabaceira, where the hike begins. *Opposite the church, follow a dirt track to the left into the valley of* Ribeira Grande. On the edge of the ➍ upland plateau you can gaze down the gorge with the rustling sugar cane and swaying palm trees. *First follow a steep 200m descent and then continue on a flat section.* You may catch sight of colourful kingfishers between the trees or even a green parrot or monkeys *(Chlorocebus).* Countless mango trees provide shade (the fruit ripens between June and September), the wind whispers in the tall sugar cane and you can hear the rushing of water. *At the bottom follow the dry stream bed to the left.* After about an hour you will see a gigantic baobab tree, several hundred

➊ **Praia**

11km   25 mins

➋ **Fortaleza Real de São Filipe**

4km   10 mins

➌ **Calabaceira**

1km   10 mins

➍ **Upland plateau**

3km   2 hrs

years old. Why not stop here for a photo? After another half hour you will reach the first foothills of Cidade Velha ➤ p. 72.

A LAND STEEPED IN HISTORY

⑤ Convento de São Francisco

0.5km   10 mins

On your right, not all that easy to see, is the ⑤ Convento de São Francisco. This monastery, built in 1640, was designed to train priests who were supposed to form a solid moral base for a local population that would have a strong Catholic faith and be obedient to their Portuguese masters. However, the attempt failed when the Portuguese started families with their African slaves and behaved immorally in all kinds of other ways. In the end, the monastic buildings were reduced to ruins. Today tourists are attracted to their interesting architecture, and the fact that the ruins were left unrestored gives them an added charm. *In order to get to the other monuments, follow the course of the stream into the village.*

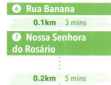

⑥ Rua Banana

0.1km   3 mins

⑦ Nossa Senhora do Rosário

0.2km   5 mins

To your right you will see a few small houses above the streambed. *Climb up the stone steps in between the houses until you reach the* ⑥ Rua Banana. From here, you can already spot the church of ⑦ Nossa Senhora do Rosário, the oldest Catholic church outside Europe. *A few old stone steps lead you down to a street that runs parallel to Rua Banana. At the bottom of the steps take a right and follow the street until it reaches the main street. Then head on to the main square,* where you can

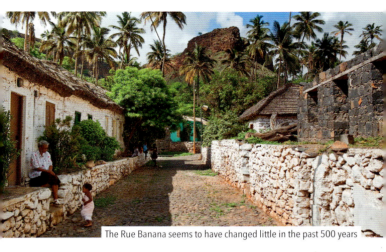

The Rue Banana seems to have changed little in the past 500 years

have a look at the ❽ Pelourinho (pillories), where criminals were once punished and slaves were sold.

LUNCH WITH A VIEW OF THE SEAFARER'S BAY

Have your lunch in ❾ Penedinho *(daily | €),* the left-hand restaurant of the two that are right by the ocean and offer a glorious view along with their food. You are looking at the bay where once upon a time Columbus and Vasco da Gama dropped anchor and Francis Drake loaded booty onto his ships. Charles Darwin also visited in 1832. Try the speciality of the house, the delicious fish soup with rice and coconut milk *(caldo de peixe).* Suitably fortified, *take the road on the right out of the village.* After around 200m you'll see the ruins of the ❿ Sé Catedral on the left. You can walk around the remains of the walls and pillars. *On the street, hail an aluguer leaving the village and ensure before boarding that it is going to Praia.* At its final stop, the ⓫ sucupira ➤ p. 71 in Praia, take a taxi back to your hotel..

INSIDER TIP
Fish & coconut

❽ Pelourinho

0.1km · 2 mins

❾ Penedinho

0.3km · 15 mins

❿ Sé Catedral

13km · 25 mins

⓫ Sucupira

❷ FOGO: EXCURSION TO A LUNAR LANDSCAPE

- ➤ Explore black-lava avalanches
- ➤ Gaze into the mouth of the volcano
- ➤ (Almost) reach the stars

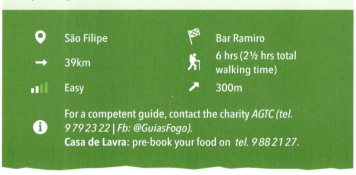

📍	São Filipe	🏁	Bar Ramiro
➜	39km	🚶	6 hrs (2½ hrs total walking time)
📶	Easy	↗	300m

ℹ For a competent guide, contact the charity *AGTC (tel. 979 23 22 | Fb: @GuiasFogo)*.
Casa de Lavra: pre-book your food on *tel. 988 21 27*.

A WINDING ROAD TO A BIZARRE WORLD

❶ **São Filipe**

28km 60 mins

❷ **Parque Natural do Fogo**

4km 45 mins

Take a taxi from your hotel in ❶ São Filipe ➤ p. 78 *to Chã das Caldeiras* ➤ p. 80. The route winds gently upwards through undulating hills, where gaping eroded fissures slice through the bare mountainside. A fabulous view opens up over the broad, hilly plain down to the ocean. Black scree and lumps of clinker increasingly dominate the landscape. Then you get your first glimpse of the lava flows: from a distance they look like broad, dark rivulets, but up close they turn out to be bizarre avalanches of rock as tall as a man.

After a final bend you find yourself in front of the wooden sign of the ❷ Parque Natural do Fogo where you can see the perfectly formed cone of the Pico do Fogo ➤ p. 81. Children sell aromatic pink pepper and carved souvenirs made of lava rock. Why not buy a small item from them? After a photo stop you drive on into the strange caldera landscape to the spot where, in 2014, the road was swallowed up by the lava.

PHOTOGENIC LAVA SCULPTURES

Here your guide awaits you in order to take you safely through the fresh lava, while your luggage is transported to your accommodation by taxi. You wade into the black lunar landscape, *400m up the gentle slopes of ash* to the ❸ Pico 2014 ➤ p. 81. Here, you look into the wide-open mouth of the volcano and can sniff its sulphurous fumes! *Then descend into the valley basin of* Chã das Caldeiras ➤ p. 80 *and take a walk through the bizarre lava fields to* Portela. This area is great for taking photographs, with new exciting scenery appearing around every bend of the track. In the spot where after the 2014 eruption only a few roof terraces and crumbled walls of former homes were visible, now a small village has reappeared. Your guide will take you to the ❹ Casa de Lavra *(€)* where your host Cecílio and his wife Elena, who is a marvellous cook, will look after you.

❸ **Pico 2014**

4km 2 hrs

❹ **Casa de Lavra**

0.3km 5 mins

DANCE UNDER THE STARS

If you aren't going to stay overnight in the Casa de Lavra, Cecílio will advise you where to find accommodation. Now it is time for a rest. Around 5pm to 5.30pm you

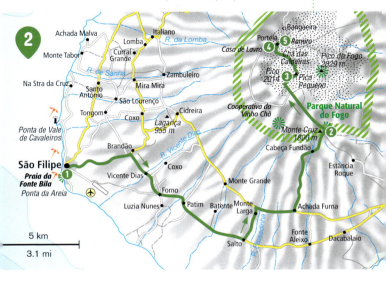

should leave for ⑤ Bar Ramiro ➤ p. 85. Ramiro and his band of musicians are famous, and his bar is always full of life. If you are brave enough, try the home-made *manecom* wine which can taste either sweet and delicious or like vinegar, depending on the year.

After your supper, which you can pre-order in your accommodation, have a close look at the sky. When it is entirely dark, Cape Verde has one of the best star skies in the world!

❸ SANTO ANTÃO: VERDANT TROPICAL PARADISE

- ➤ **Enjoy breathtaking views from a height**
- ➤ **Hike on ancient mule tracks**
- ➤ **Taste fresh Cape Verde coffee**

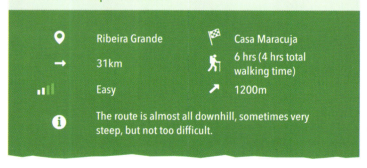

📍 Ribeira Grande	🏁 Casa Maracuja
→ 31km	🥾 6 hrs (4 hrs total walking time)
📶 Easy	↗ 1200m
ℹ The route is almost all downhill, sometimes very steep, but not too difficult.	

① **Ribeira Grande**

8km　20 mins

② **Delgadim**

12km　40 mins

ASCEND TO DIZZYING HEIGHTS

From ① Ribeira Grande ➤ p. 97 *make your way up to the Cova-Crater by taxi.* During the trip along the old, cobbled road you will get to enjoy plenty of breathtaking views, but none of them compare to the dizzying chasms that await at ② Delgadim ➤ p. 96. Then the road winds steeply upwards to almost 1,400m, where fine, silver-green lichen hang from the tree branches. Finally, on the left you will see the collapsed circular crater of Cova do Paúl. Behind the crater, turn off left onto a narrow, paved road and follow it to the end.

THROUGH THE CLOUD FOREST

Your hike begins at the ❸ **end of the cobbled road**. *A path to your right winds its way past a few little houses, first to the left and then to the right, to the crater wall.* You need about 20 minutes to reach the peak of ❹ **Cova do Paúl ➤ p. 96**. If the weather is clear, enjoy a spectacular view: Ribeira do Paúl ➤ **p. 98** zigzags 6km down to the ocean. *From here, there is a paved mule path that goes steeply downhill in tight turns.* It passes through a cloud forest, past lava fields full of impressive boulders, then through rattling sugar cane fields and coffee plantations. In the little village of **Cabo da Ribeira** you will see a sign on the right that reads: ❺ **Chez Sandro ➤ p. 100**. Here there are local handicrafts and freshly brewed Santo Antão coffee.

HOME-GROWN ORGANIC LETTUCE

It is about another 20-minute walk to the village where you'll have lunch. In ❻ **O Curral ➤ p. 99** Christine will spoil you with freshly baked bread and other home-made specialities, including the tastiest organic lettuce from her own garden and the purest *grogue* in the entire archipelago. With renewed strength, carry on walking: *the road continues downhill for another 5km, past banana plants, mighty mango trees and coconut palms.* Now and again you will see hidden houses with straw roofs, and occasionally a rare dragon tree. *Walk through Eito to* **Cidade das Pombas ➤ p. 97**. Tired but satisfied – you've finally reached your destination – you really deserve to treat yourself to a delicious passion fruit pontche on the rooftop terrace of the ❼ **Casa Maracuja ➤ p. 99**, before taking a taxi to your accommodation.

INSIDER TIP
Lovely lettuce

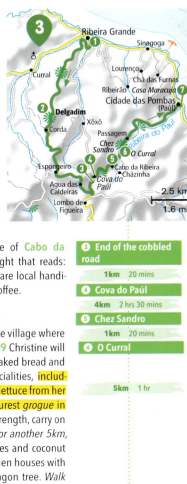

2.5 km
1.6 mi

❸ **End of the cobbled road**

| 1km | 20 mins |

❹ **Cova do Paúl**

| 4km | 2 hrs 30 mins |

❺ **Chez Sandro**

| 1km | 20 mins |

❻ **O Curral**

| 5km | 1 hr |

❼ **Casa Maracuja**

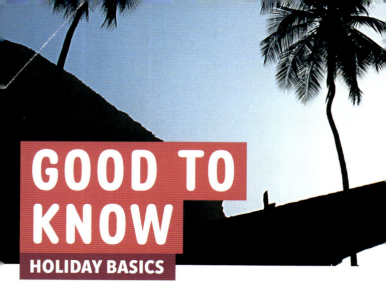

GOOD TO KNOW
HOLIDAY BASICS

ARRIVAL

GETTING THERE

To date, there are four international airports in Cape Verde: on the islands of Sal (SID), Boa Vista (BVC), Santiago (RAI) and São Vicente (VXE). From the UK there are direct flights to Sal and Boa Vista with Tui *(www.tui.co.uk/flight)* while from the United States the popular route is via Lisbon where there are regular direct flights with the Portuguese national airline TAP *(flytap.com)* and with Cabo Verde Airlines *(caboverdeairlines.com)* from Lisbon to Sal, Santiago and São Vicente several times a week.

GETTING IN

Since 2019 there has been no requirement to obtain a visa to enter the country. Instead, the so-called Airport Security Tax (AST) has been introduced.

 – 2 hours in summer

–1 hour behind
–2 hours in summer

You need to register on the government's website *ease.gov.cv* at least five days before you want to enter the country. You need the following details in order to do so: ID, travel dates, contact number and the first hotel of your stay. The fee of 3,400 CVE (30.83 euros) must be paid by credit card.

 Adapter Type C

You will need a European adapter type C

A man and his son walk along *a levada (*water channel) on Santo Antão

CLIMATE & WHEN TO GO

The dry tropical climate makes Cape Verde an ideal year-round holiday destination. On average there are 350 days of sunshine a year, with temperatures between 21°C and 29°C. January and February are the coolest and windiest months and it is particularly hot in August and September. During this period there are often heavy tropical downpours but the trade winds are less strong from July to October. There is only around 5°C difference between day and night temperatures. The water temperature ranges from 22–27°C.

GETTING AROUND

CAR HIRE

Cars can be hired on almost all the islands. However, the roads, conditions and driving habits might take some getting used to and the time and costs involved (high deposit) are significant. It is possible to hire a taxi or *aluguer*, with a local driver who knows his way around, for the same price as a hired car.

DOMESTIC FLIGHTS

With the exception of Santo Antão and Brava, all the islands are served by ATR turboprop aircraft. Domestic flights are offered by BestFly Cabo Verde (TICV) *(bestflycaboverde.com)* and by Cabo Verde Airlines *(caboverdeairlines. com)*.

FERRIES

The ferry from São Vicente to Santo Antão is reliable and departs several times daily; there is a ferry connection to Brava (approx. 30 minutes) several times a week. There are sporadic initiatives to connect other islands by ferry. For example, ferries to São Nicolau may be highly reliable for several months, only to be suspended for a while, and so on. *cvinterilhas.cv*

PUBLIC TRANSPORT

⚑ *Aluguers* travel between the larger towns and connect villages with the next major communities. Ask where these shared taxis start from or flag one down on the road. Short trips cost around 100 CVE; the drivers have an official price list for all routes.

There are also regular bus services in the town centre and suburbs of Mindelo and Praia. This can be ideal for a city tour: in Mindelo, all regular buses are on a *volta*, which means that you are able to exit in the same location where you started your journey.

The most scenic line is No. 10. In the capital Praia take line 4, 5, 6, 8 or 9. The driver (who sometimes turns DJ!) is entitled to charge you again for the return trip; even so, you still pay less than 100 CVE!

TAXIS

The trip from the airports in São Vicente, Praia and Sal to the city centre or capital costs around 1,000 CVE (9 euros) during the day; a small surcharge is added at night. There are fixed rates in the cities: a trip in the city area of Mindelo costs 150 CVE during the day (200 CVE at night), for example; in the centre of Praia 150–200 CVE during the day (200–300 at night).

EMERGENCIES

CONSULATES & EMBASSIES

There is no British Embassy in Cape Verde. If in urgent need of consular assistance, contact the British Embassy in Lisbon, Portugal or the British Embassy in Dakar, Senegal.

BRITISH EMBASSY LISBON, PORTUGAL

Rua de São Bernardo 33 | 1249-082 Lisbon | tel. +351 21 392 40 00 or +44 20 7008 5000 | www.gov.uk/ world/organisations/british-embassy-lisbon

BRITISH EMBASSY DAKAR, SENEGAL

BP 6025 Dakar | tel. +221 33 868 60

FESTIVALS & EVENTS
ALL YEAR ROUND

FEBRUARY
Carnival (all islands): especially São Vicente, see p. 111, São Nicolau, see p. 119). See photo

MARCH/APRIL
Grito Rock Praia (Santiago): music festival. *FB*

APRIL
Kriol Jazz Festival (Santiago): see p. 76
Santiago Music Expo (Santiago): music festival. *Atlanticmusicexpo.com*

APRIL/MAY
Festa de Nhô Filipe (Fogo): days around 1 May, see p. 84

MAY
Festival Manuel Gamboa (Santiago): 19 May, see p. 76

JUNE
Festa de São João (all islands): especially Nhô San Jon in Porto Novo on Santo Antão, 24 June, see p. 104

JULY
Festa de Santa Isabel (Boa Vista), 4 July, see p. 58
Festival da Praia de Areia Grande (Santiago): music festival

AUGUST
Festival Baía das Gatas (São Vicente): first full moon weekend, see p. 111
Festival Praia d'Tedja (São Nicolau): music festival
Festival Pedra de Lume (Sal): music festival
Festival de Curraletes (Santo Antão): music festival

SEPTEMBER
Festival Internacional de Santa Maria (Sal): 15 September, see p. 51
Mindelact (São Vicente): see p. 112

OCTOBER/NOVEMBER
Festival 7 Sóis, 7 Luas: international festival of culture with events on Santo Antão, Santiago, Fogo, Brava, Maio. *festival7sois.eu*

31 or +44 20 7008 5000 | *www.gov. uk/government/world/organisations/ british-embassy-dakar*

ESSENTIALS

US EMBASSY

Rua Abilio Macedo 6 | Praia, Cape Verde | tel. +238 260 8900 | cv.us embassy.gov

EMERGENCY SERVICES

Police: tel. 1 32; Ambulance: tel. 1 30; Fire brigade: tel. 1 31

HEALTH

There are chemists and clinics *(centro de saúde)* where a nurse or aid is available 24 hours a day on all the islands and there are state hospitals on Santiago, São Vicente, Santo Antão, Fogo and Sal. There is a considerable amount of bureaucracy and waiting times are long. Private clinics are a convenient alternative for holiday-makers, and communication is often also easier. Chemists can be identified by a sign with a green cross and they usually stock the most commonly used medicines. In spite of this, you should have a first-aid kit with you: good sunscreen, mosquito repellent, pain relief and stomach settling medication are always a good idea.

National health schemes will not usually meet the cost of treatment so it is advisable to take out private health insurance.

ACCOMMODATION

The eastern islands, which have been developed for tourism, have large hotels to European standards. On the mountainous islands you find predominantly smaller guesthouses *(pensão/residêncial)* or private rooms of varying standards.

ADDRESSES

Not all of the streets have names – not even in the larger towns – and those that do often don't have numbers. Addresses often only consist of the district or a nearby reference point.

CUSTOMS

The import and export of local currency is prohibited. The import of foreign currency is unlimited, subject to declaration on arrival and on departure. The export of foreign currency is limited to the equivalent of CVE 20,000 or the amount declared on arrival, whichever is the larger.

Duty free allowance includes the import of 200 cigarettes, 1 litre of spirits and items intended for your personal use, such as perfume.

Travellers returning to the UK do not have to pay duty on articles purchased overseas up to the value of £390, but there are limits on quantities of alcohol and tobacco products. For details, please refer to *www.gov. uk/bringing-goods-into-uk-personal-use*. US citizens should refer to *www. cbp.gov*.

DRINKING WATER

Tap water is not suitable for drinking and you should also use bottled water to brush your teeth. Check that the bottled water you are served in restaurants is still sealed.

LANGUAGE

The official language in Cape Verde is Portuguese, but in their daily lives, people speak Cape Verdean Creole (*Kriolu*), although even visitors are able to hear a difference in dialect between the leeward islands (*Sotavento*) and the windward ones (*Barlavento*). On Santo Antão and São Vicente many people speak French, whereas English is spoken on Fogo and Brava.

MEDIA

Radio is a very popular pastime in Cape Verde – about 80 per cent of the residents listen to it every day. Most broadcasts are in Portuguese, but there are also some regional stations that broadcast in Creole.

The two big national newspapers *A Semana* and *Expresso das Ilhas* are published weekly in Portuguese. If you are looking for international newspapers and magazines you can try your luck at the international airports.

MONEY & CREDIT CARDS

The currency is the Cape Verdean escudo (CVE). Its exchange rate is fixed to the euro (1 euro = 110.27 CVE).

Increasingly, the euro is accepted for purchases, but at a rate of 1 euro = 100 CVE. ATMs have a limit of 20,000

CVE (181 euros) per withdrawal, and most cards only allow you to withdraw once a day. In an emergency, you can get larger amounts in a bank *(Mon–Fri 8am–3pm)*, but you will pay high service charges and may have to queue for half a day! If you don't want to go through this kind of trouble, buy your next bottle in one of the bigger supermarkets, e.g. Kalu & Angela (Praia): Fragata (Mindelo) and pay with a larger euro note. The cashier may hesitate at first, but eventually your note will be accepted and you'll get the change in escudos that you were looking for.

INSIDER TIP
How to get change

HOW MUCH DOES IT COST?

Water	1 euro for a 1.5-litre bottle in the mini mercado
Coffee	1 euro for an espresso
Aluguer	3.50 euros for a journey from Porto Novo to Ponta do Sol
Snack	2.50 euros for a sandwich/ cachupa
Guide	from 35 euros for half a day
Surfboard	10 euros rental per hour

NOISE

Don't forget to pack earplugs. The noise from the street, especially in city

The local women often carry very heavy loads on their heads

centres, can be very annoying late at night and early in the morning. Dogs barking all night long is the rule, not the exception.

OPENING HOURS
Shops are open Monday to Friday 8am–12.30pm and 3–6.30pm and Saturday 8am–1pm (plus/minus half an hour). They are closed on Sunday and public holidays.

PHOTOGRAPHS
As always, good manners dictate that you should ask permission before taking photographs of people. Women, in particular, don't react kindly to being photographed without their permission!

POST
There is a post office with a red sign (*Correios de Cabo Verde*) in all major towns where you can purchase stamps, phone cards, make telephone calls (expensive) and post your letters. Postal charges for a letter or a postcard to Europe are 60 CVE. Opening hours (*as a rule, Mon-Fri 9am-1pm and 3-5pm*) can vary.

PUBLIC HOLIDAYS
1 Jan	New Year
20 Jan	National Heroes' Day
March/April	Good Friday
1 May	Labour Day
24 June	São João
5 July	Independence Day
15 Aug	Assumption Day
12 Sept	National Day
1 Nov	All Saints' Day
25 Dec	Christmas Day

SWIMMING
Don't underestimate the rough surf and strong currents at many beaches. Never go swimming completely on your own, stay at designated beaches and pay attention to the flags: green = safe to swim; yellow = restricted swimming permitted; red = swimming prohibited.

Nudism is not just unknown in Cape Verde but it is prohibited.

TELEPHONE & WIFI
Many European providers have roaming contracts with one of the Cape Verdean telecom companies (CV Móvel, Unitel T+). However, costs are not capped and can quickly add up. Therefore, a local SIM card can be

useful, not just for making telephone calls but also for mobile internet.

The country code for Cape Verde is +238 followed by the seven-digit telephone number. When making a call from Cape Verde, dial +44 for the UK and +1 for the US and Canada.

Free WiFi can be found at most airports, at central locations in big cities or near the post office, as well as in many cafés, restaurants and hotels.

TIPPING

A tip of five to ten per cent is appropriate in restaurants if you are satisfied with the service. For a small tip, porters are available to help you at the ports and airports.

TOILETS

Due to the use of narrow waste-water pipes and low water pressure, in most locations you need to put the loo paper in buckets that are provided.

TOURIST INFORMATION

The official tourist information website is *turismo.cv*. However, quite often your hotel will be better informed about current happenings. In Praia, Tarrafal (Santiago), Mindelo and Porto Novo, local information desks should be able to give you good advice.

WEATHER ON SAL

High season
Low season

	JAN	FEB	MARCH	APRIL	MAY	JUNE	JULY	AUG	SEPT	OCT	NOV	DEC
Daytime temperature	24°	23°	23°	25°	26°	27°	28°	29°	30°	28°	27°	25°
Night-time temperature	19°	19°	20°	20°	20°	22°	23°	24°	25°	23°	22°	21°
Hours of sunshine per day	8	9	10	10	10	8	7	6	8	8	9	8
Rainy days per month	1	1	1	0	0	2	3	3	4	3	1	1
Sea temperature in °C	22	23	24	24	25	26	27	27	27	27	25	23

☀ Hours of sunshine per day   🌧 Rainy days per month   ≈ Sea temperature in °C

WORDS & PHRASES
IN KRIOLU

yes/no/perhaps	**sim/nau/talvez**
please	**fabor**
thank you	**obrigádu**
Good morning/day/evening/night	**Bom diâ!/Bo tárdi!/Bo noti!**
Hello!/Goodbye!	**Olâ!/Tchau!**
My name is …	**M-tchoma …**
What's your name?	**Módi bu tchoma?**
I am from …	**Mi é di …**
Excuse me!	**Diskulpâ-m!**
Pardon?	**Módi**
I (don't) like this.	**M-(ka) gosta.**
I would like …/I am looking for …	**M-kré …/M-sata djobi …**
Where can I find internet access?	**La pundi um podi usa interneti?/ interneti sem fio?**

SYMBOLS

EATING & DRINKING

Could you please book a table for tonight for four?	Riserva um mesa pa kuátu alguém pa oxi, fabor.
Could I please have …? salt/pepper/sugar	M-ta toma …? sal/margéta/sukri
bottle/glass	garáfa/kópui
with/without	ku/sem
ice/sparkling	gélu/okisijenádu
vegetarian/allergy	ka kumi kárni/alerjiâ
May I have the bill, please?	Tarsê-m kónta, fabor.
bill/receipt	kónta/risibu
cash/credit card	em notas/kartom vinti-kuátu
supermarket/grocery store	supermerkádu/lója
bakery	padariâ

MISCELLANEOUS

Where is …/are …?	Undi sta …?
Do you speak Kriolu?	Bu ta papia Kriolu?
How much is …? today/tomorrow/yesterday	… é kántu? oxi/manham/ónti
Monday/Tuesday/Wednesday/ Thursday/Friday/Saturday/	Sugunda-fera/Térsa-fera/Kuárta-fera/Kinta-fera/Sésta-fera/Sábru/
Sunday	Diâ Dimingu
open/closed	abertu/fexadu
right/left/straight ahead	ndreta/skérda/frenti
more/less	más/más poku
cheap/expensive	barátu/káru
too much/a lot/too little	dimas/um munti/un poku
ticket	bilieti
Help!/Watch out!	Sakor!/Kutádu!
danger/dangerous	pirigusu
forbidden/banned	pruibidu
(no) drinking water	(ka) águ bebi
fever/pain	fébri/dor
pharmacy	formása
breakdown/garage	bariâ/ofisina
broken/doesn't work	stragádu
0/1/2/3/4/5/6/7/8/9/10/100/1,000	zéru/um/dós/trés/kuátu/sinku/séx/séti/oitu/nóvi/dés/sem/mil

HOLIDAY VIBES

FOR RELAXATION & CHILLING

FOR BOOKWORMS & FILM BUFFS

📖 THE LAST WILL & TESTAMENT OF SENHOR DA SILVA ARAÚJO (1989)

This humorous portrait of Cape Verdean society by Germano Almeida (translated by Sheila Faria Glaser) tells the tale of Senhor da Silva's rise from poverty to prosperous businessman. The book was made into a film (*Napomuceno's Will*) by Francisco Manso in 1997.

📖 CAPE VERDE: CRIOULO COLONY TO INDEPENDENT NATION (1995)

Richard Lobban's fascinating study of Cape Verde's history from the slave trade to independence explores the country's cultural heritage, economics and politics (Westview Press).

📖 TRANSNATIONAL ARCHIPELAGO: PERSPECTIVES ON CAPE VERDEAN MIGRATION & DIASPORA (2008)

Edited by Luís Batalha and Jørgen Carling, this study explores subjects such as language and music, and the impact of the Cape Verdean diaspora.

📹 TCHINDAS (2015)

Written and directed by Pablo García Pérez de Lara and Marc Serena, this multi-award-winning documentary is the portrait of a community on Cape Verde as it is prepares for Carnival. The central figure is a transgender woman who is beloved and respected within the community and who leads the preparations for the celebration.

PLAYLIST

0:58

⏸ **CESÁRIA ÉVORA – SODADE**
Arguably the best-known interpretation of the famous classic.

▶ **MIRRI LOBO – ENCOMENDA DE TERRA**
Ideal for getting into the mood or for soothing your *sodade* after you return home.

▶ **NEUZA – DJAR FOGO**
A hymn to the island of Fogo.

▶ **BANA – FITCHI FATCHI NA TRACOLANÇA**
One of Bana's hits features gossip Cape Verde style.

▶ **LURA – NA RI NA**
Lura is not the only one, but is currently the best-known successor of the great Cesária.

▶ **CORDAS DO SOL – COMPED JOAQUIM**
Fans from Brava to Boston have loved this band for many years.

Your holiday soundtrack can be found on **Spotify** under **MARCO POLO Cape Verde**

Or scan this code with the Spotify app

ONLINE

A SWEET PAIN – THE REBEL SYNTHS OF CABO VERDE

A short film about an incredible story in Cape Verdean music: in 1968 a cargo ship full of brand-new synthesizers and keyboards ran aground off São Nicolau. Amílcar Cabral had the equipment distributed in local schools, thereby inspiring a new generation of musicians. *short.travel/kav14*

AYO GAME

Oril as an app: a simple way to get along with local people.

CAPEVERDETIPS.CO.UK

A site that provides some very useful travel information about visas, flights, travel between the islands, hotels and medical facilities. It also has an extensive photo gallery and much more.

OCEAN BLOGS – CAPE VERDE

If you have always wanted to know how marine scientists work, follow the daily life of the German Geomar Centre and the Cape Verdean Ocean Science Center Mindelo, off Cape Verde (in English). *oceanblogs.org/capeverde*

TRAVEL PURSUIT

THE MARCO POLO HOLIDAY QUIZ

Do you know your facts about Cape Verde? Here you can test your knowledge of the little secrets and idiosyncrasies of the country and its people. You will find the correct answers below, with further details on pages 20 to 25 of this guide.

❶ What is an *aluguer*?
a) A bush taxi
b) A shared taxi
c) A day taxi

❷ Which faith is most widespread in Cape Verde?
a) Adventism
b) Islam
c) Catholicism

❸ What is the term for melancholic weariness?
a) Solande
b) Sodade
c) Monade

❹ Which animal is used for transporting water?
a) Donkey
b) Camel
c) Mule

❺ Which group of islands is home to the *rabelados?*
a) Fogo
b) Boa vista
c) Santiago

❻ What is the name of a type of traditional Cape Verdean music?
a) Funana
b) Bachata
c) Maracatu

Correct answers: 1b, 2c, 3b, 4a, 5c, 6a, 7a, 8b, 9a, 10a, 11c, 12b

Spoiler alert! (question 1): the *aluguer* is the most popular means of public transport

❼ How many passengers fit into an *aluguer*?
a) 15
b) 17
c) 23

❽ What is the Cape Verdean national language?
a) Criolin
b) Kriolu
c) Kriolé

❾ Education is compulsory until which grade?
a) Year 6
b) Year 8
c) Year 10

❿ What is *grogue*?
a) Sugar cane rum
b) Fruit punch
c) Pomace liqueur

⓫ What is Cape Verde's official language?
a) Spanish
b) French
c) Portuguese

⓬ Who is Cape Verde's most famous musician?
a) Carmen Souza
b) Cesária Évora
c) Sara Tavares

INDEX

WE WANT TO HEAR FROM YOU!

Did you have a great holiday? Is there something on your mind? Whatever it is, let us know! Whether you want to praise the guide, alert us to errors or give us a personal tip – MARCO POLO would be pleased to hear from you. Please contact us by email:

We do everything we can to provide the very latest information for your trip. Nevertheless, despite all of our authors' thorough research, errors can creep in. MARCO POLO does not accept any liability for this.

sales@heartwoodpublishing.co.uk

PICTURE CREDITS
Cover photo: Sal, Buracona, Vulkan (Schapowalow: R. Spila)
Photos: DuMont Bildarchiv: Schwarzbach (Klappe innen/1, 22); Getty Images/Lonely Planet Images: J. Borthwick (60); huber-images: Schmid (8/9, 50/51, 72, 74, 92/93), R. Schmid (back inside flap, 14/15, 24, 100, 106); Laif: M. Riehle (30), G. Stand (120); Laif/Explorer: P. Le Floch (54); Laif/Hemis: F. Guiziou (46, 97); Laif/hemis.fr: P. Hauser (16/17, 52); Laif/Le Figaro Magazine: Fautre (109), S. Fautre (66/67, 123); Laif/photo alto: L. Mouton (33); Look: H. Dressler (80), U. Wiesmeier (128/129); Look/age fotostock (111); mauritius images/Alamy (28, 32, 40/41, 86, 105, 131), J. Cabral (45), M. Wakem (11); mauritius images/Andia/Alamy (85); mauritius images/Arterra Picture Library/Alamy (103); mauritius images/Hemis. fr: R. Mattes (6/7); mauritius images/imageBROKER: R. Bordoni (10); mauritius images/Masterfile/Siephoto (118); mauritius images/Photononstop: N. Thibaut (99); H. Mielke (12, 34/35, 59, 63, 65, 79, 114, 134); picture alliance/imageBROKER: R. Bordoni (71); D. Renckhoff (37, 49); A. Rieck (89, 90/91, 143); Schapowalow: R. Schmid (82), R. Spila (2/3); Shutterstock: S. Aznar (26/27, 57, 140/141), gg-foto/Shutterstock (6-7), lcdpstock/Shutterstock (20), D. Gross (138/139); Shutterstock/Samuel Borges Photography (front outer and inside flap, 1); T. Stankiewicz (21, 76/77, 112/113, 117); vario images/imagebroker (13); vario images/unlisted images (29).

3rd Edition – fully revised and updated 2023
Worldwide Distribution: Heartwood Publishing Ltd, Bath, United Kingdom
www.heartwoodpublishing.co.uk

Authors: Annette Rieck
Editor: Ulrike Frühwald
Picture editor: Stefanie Wiese
Cartography: © MAIRDUMONT, Ostfildern (pp. 38–39, 122, 125, 127, outside jacket, pull-out map); © MAIRDUMONT, Ostfildern, using data from OpenStreetMap, licence CC-BY-SA 2.0 (pp. 42–43, 68–69, 94–95)
Cover design and pull-out map cover design: bilekjaeger_Kreativagentur with Zukunftswerkstatt, Stuttgart
Page design: Langenstein Communication GmbH, Ludwigsburg

Heartwood Publishing credits:
Translated from the German by Thomas Moser, Robert McInnes and Lisa Davey
Editors: Felicity Laughton, Kate Michell, Sophie Blacksell Jones
Prepress: Summerlane Books, Bath
Printed in India

MARCO POLO AUTHOR
ANNETTE RIECK
People tend to ask journalist and hiking guide Annette three questions: How did you get here? By plane! How long have you been living in Cape Verde? For 12 years! What do you live on? Air, love and hard work! Any more questions?

DOS & DON'TS

HOW TO AVOID SLIP-UPS & BLUNDERS

DO AVOID BUYING TURTLE PRODUCTS
Never buy any souvenirs or other products derived from turtles. They always cost the life of one of the few existing animals. And, most governments also prohibit their import, making it illegal for you to take them home.

DON'T UNDERESTIMATE THE SUN
At these latitudes, the sun is so intense that it can be a real danger for pale skin. And the constant breeze eases the heat but increases the risk of sunburn. Always use a sunscreen with a high protection factor – even if it is cloudy. And always take a hat.

DO EXPECT A RELAXED ATTITUDE TOWARDS TIME
Some things on Cape Verde are fundamentally different, and one such example is the approach to time. An hour earlier or later, or a day more or less is not so important. You should leave any expectations you have about punctuality at home.

DON'T WASTE WATER
Local people are used to making the most of every drop of this precious commodity, whereas holidaymakers often consume 20 times the amount of water. Save water whenever you can!